RICHANAH DALY

drawing YOUR GOAL CLOSER

AN ART-BASED APPROACH TO VISUALISING YOUR GOALS AND MAKING THEM A REALITY

Cover image by: Lumi Lumi Visuals, 99Designs
Book design by: SWATT Books Ltd
Editing and proofreading: Craig Smith (CRS Editorial)

Printed in the United Kingdom
First Printed 2022

ISBN: 978-1-7395893-0-1 (Paperback)
ISBN: 978-1-7395893-1-8 (eBook)

Richanah Daly
Halesowen, West Midlands

richanah.co.uk

Contents

Introduction: The Influence of Art on Me . . . .

Chapter 1: Why Get Creative? . . . .

Chapter 2: The TARGET Model . . . .

Chapter 3: T = Talent: Your Own Tree of Strength . . . .

Chapter 4: A = Aim: Mapping Your Aspirational Goal . . . .

Chapter 5: R = Reality: Where Are You Right Now? . . . .

Chapter 6: G = Growth: Turning Obstacles into Opportunities .

Chapter 7: E = Evaluation: Taking a Moment to Reflect on
This New Perspective . . . .

Chapter 8: T = Timeline: Stepping Stones and Action Plan . .

Summary: Your Big Picture: Bringing it All Together . . . . . .

Templates . . . .

My Story: Driven by Adversity and Life Learnings . . . .

About the Author . . . .

Acknowledgements . . . .

Introduction
The Influence of Art on Me

I've always been a visual thinker. My earliest memory of recognising this as a way of expression was back when I went to playgroup at around the age of three. Apparently, the paints and easels were my area of choice when it came to free time and messy play (why the other children had fascinations with the sandpit or dolls seemed a bit odd to me!). Here, in front of me, were an array of colours and a blank canvas. This is where you can create anything you desire... it's so open and free!

Needless to say, our home was littered with paintings. I couldn't wait to bring home my creations; all of which were greeted by my Mom with the same wonder and surprise.

My Mom is an extremely talented artist. Drawing and painting have always come natural to her, so I've had a wonderfully supportive and encouraging environment to explore creativity. One notable trait within all my paintings at an early age was the presence of a rainbow. I recall being asked by my schoolteachers what it meant to always have a rainbow present. For me, it was simple... because it has all the colours in it. None are left out! Colour has always been immensely important to me as it has feeling and energy, which, as I found out in my early 20s when I started sensing auras in people, can signify connections. These connections can be insightful as to how we may be feeling or thinking, or our outlook.

So, why am I telling you this? Well, the link with colour and expression through visuals becomes more and more powerful, especially when we consider future goals and aspirations. The fact that the future is not yet here brings magic, hope, potential and the opportunity to shape our own destiny.

Equally, getting ideas out of our heads and onto paper is a fantastic self-reflective form of expression. I'm always drawn to abstract art for this reason (pun intended)!

What if I told you that you can coach yourself by creating your own images, from your imagination and instinct, to help you navigate your pathway to success? Exciting, right?!

*It is a myth that you have to be good
at drawing to be an artist.*

You really don't!

You just need to allow yourself to explore, be curious and experiment. Sure, it helps if this embraces your talent, which is brilliant if you are an artist, but it isn't an essential requirement to appreciate this book, or the coaching model introduced. If a traditional 'stick person' is your limit or your comfort zone, then don't fear – I am a big fan of stick people drawings!

There have been times in my life where I have parked the 'arty' side to focus my attention on work, or at least the work that focuses outside of an artist's space. Even up to about 12 months ago I had decided that unless I do a job where I can use this skill, then it's pointless to incorporate it into the workplace as it has no relevance or significance. **Wrong again!**

Over the last couple of years I've felt myself thinking differently, partly due to having an exceptional line manager (Emma) who fully embraced the individuality of all her team members and allowed me the space to be my full creative self. 'I want you to bring your whole self to work' she would urge. She wanted to understand the true me; the many layers and levels. This is a leadership quality of Emma's I have particularly admired.

This was also the lady who encouraged that when it came to continuous professional development or my performance development plan, these were created in an authentic way that played to my strengths and true style. So, I'd ditch the Excel spreadsheet and opt for pens and paper, or my tablet, to draw out my direction and objectives. I've always found tables and spreadsheets quite restrictive when detailing my passions. After all, how free can you be when confined to the parameters of a box or grid?

This was such a liberating experience, and one that enabled me to feel fully valued for just being me. Not only that, but it excited me as to the content I was going to put in. I would tune into my hopeful, aspirational and curious self, back to when I was three years old. So much potential yet to be uncovered, and I am the storyteller, the composer, through images and colour.

I knew there was something to this method of working, and surely I cannot be the only one who appreciates working beyond structured tables and words? It was when I began to study for my coaching qualification that a huge penny dropped. Visuals are a massive conversation trigger in exploration and discovery when connecting and building relationships.

So, if this is true, then potentially there's more to unlocking our creative side when trying to better understand ourselves, work out a problem or articulate something that, for whatever reason, right now, means the words are not immediately known to us.

Initially, I started unpacking my new learnings with simple (yes, honestly, they are simple) visual brainstorms. This is my version of notetaking and extracting the meaning, and how I might use this learning. I came to realise a critical point in my own career journey. Where was I going? What do I really want?

I couldn't answer these questions. I had coaching conversations and still it felt that, although there were options, nothing was really singing to me with clarity or gusto. I didn't know what I needed to do to become clear. This is where, surprisingly, I had my own little breakthrough!

I started intuitively drawing out all my options, properly connecting with each one, identifying my own strengths and the ones that were important to me. Not just the stuff I'm good at, but the things that I am energised by, which **had** to include all the 'best version of me' stuff and the 'oh my goodness, I **love** this and want to do more of it' stuff.

I spent a couple of hours creating this mind map and wont further into the detail around my own challenges and what my ideal aspirational goal looked and felt like. The more I immersed myself, the more I felt the doors in my mind unlock. I had started framing key coaching questions all around myself. I was starting to unearth some profound answers. The beauty about using creativity is when you get to leave judgement at the door and just go with the flow. It allows you to believe that there are no limits to your potential.

I felt incredibly motivated and excited to talk through and share what I had discovered with Emma and my coach, Carl, who supported me through my qualification.

I am where I am now, putting my practices into words and pictures, because of these people and their unwavering support and encouragement. Both excellent coaches with heaps of experience and credibility, they recognised a potential in me that I had pushed aside and helped me realise my own pathway.

I've since used this strength to create my own coaching model, which we will go through in Chapter 1, and I've been using it ever since with my coaching clients with fantastic results.

CREATE YOUR journey TO YOUR BIG PICTURE...

Chapter 1
Why Get Creative?

So, you might now be thinking, 'OK – so that worked for you. How do I get this to work for me, especially if I'm not an arty, creative type?' As I said earlier, **it doesn't matter**!

I have created techniques that you can either use as templates or as inspiration to go freestyle, however you choose. It's your journey, your creations, your... **you**!

We know that using visuals can enhance a coaching conversation, break the ice and delve deeper within our psyche. I am a massive fan of image cards and discussion for how a particular image resonates with me at a specific time or in an experience. Instead of holding up a deck of images to you, I am empowering you to create your own. Raw, honest, intuitive and completely yours!

All you will need to get into this is paper and either coloured pens, crayons or pastels (it's your choice). You can use an array of coloured sticky notes if you prefer. I've included some quick templates within this book, which you can replicate as a structure, so that you can focus solely on the content you are going to add.

Let me tell you why this works for those being coached. Based on the feedback I have already had from clients, they found these artistic visual techniques to be particularly powerful as they allowed them to:

- discover their potential and possibilities which were not immediately known
- focus on their own self-reflection (or introduce this as a new habit)
- gain new/different perspectives
- provide motivation through challenge
- provide their own clarity – what it was that was important to them and where they wanted to go
- explore new ways of thinking.

If we hadn't used the visual techniques during their coaching, they may not have reached the same conclusions, and if they did, it would have undoubtedly taken a lot longer.

Rather than feel pressured to have answers in response to any coaching questions I was asking, they had different ways to explore what was stopping them, holding them back, and what they held most important.

Success From My Creative Coaching Model

From what I have seen in my own coaching practice, offering alternative methods and techniques is usually very welcome, but where this has resonated well is with those who like to 'think in pictures'.

One client in particular found this model to be a breakthrough for them in their overall thinking and planning habits. Another found that it allowed them the space and freedom to explore more of their subconscious, to help them articulate what was going on in their mind more effectively.

Below are some extracts of reviews I have received from clients:

'We often forget to self-reflect on achievements and journeys throughout our working lives, but Richanah's coaching model gives you the ability to not only do that but also establish a clear path to achieve your next goal. It's visionary coaching that helps you see your true potential, which is often overlooked. It's the simplest things that have the greatest impact and this is a clear example of that.' Client A (2021)

'I have received coaching from Richanah, and it has been amazing! The way she encourages you to be creative, and the way in which the images you create guide and inform the process is both powerful and unique... I could not recommend this process highly enough.' Client B (2021)

'Using her creative exercises, I have found new ways to clearly visualise my journey.' Client C (2021)

'This has helped me so much. It has been an active coaching experience encompassing different exercises, critical conversations and actions, which has helped me thoroughly since I started coaching with Richanah.' Client D (2021)

I couldn't have felt prouder of my clients' achievements and their fantastic development journeys as they were beginning to unfold. They have been an absolute pleasure to work with and where this model helped them most is when they started to explore what coaching could do for them beyond conversations.

I was receiving a flurry of beautiful imagery into my inbox, whether digital drawings, freestyle doodles or abstract collages. These were exciting revelations that they couldn't wait to share with me. It was giving them deeper insight into their own potential in a way that they hadn't explored before. It was truly magical. It was demonstrating that an art-inspired approach to coaching was working, and what's more, they were really getting into it!

Coaching and Career Crossroads

You might be in that exact place I was a little while ago, knowing you want to develop yourself and somehow progress, but just not knowing how.

You may be one of those people who has more clarity on where you are going, which is fantastic, but you might be unsure how to get there. (Hold that thought for now, we will come onto the destination and goal, but there's still more wonderfully impactful insights to uncover beforehand.)

I always thought 'What's your goal?' or 'Where is it you want to get to?' as curious questions to appear early on in coaching conversations.

I know as a coach why these questions are fundamental and beneficial to capture early in the contracting stages of the coaching journey. The focus is all about the goal of the client; you need to be working towards something. It frames the coaching contract and all the conversations you have. But for the client, if they don't know the answers, or aren't able to articulate the answers in the conversation right there and then, it can be difficult (though not impossible) to resolve.

So, the first focus of my coaching model isn't the goal (this is actually the second stage), but it is still **very** important.

Where to Start

If you were to imagine you wanted to take an exciting journey, and you were going into a travel agent to talk about this adventure and book your tickets, what do you think the travel agent may ask you?

Yes, they will ask you where you want to go… but in order to plot your journey, book your flights etc, what else do they need to know?

Where am I going to ?...

Where am I going from ?...

That's right, 'Where are you going from?'

And it's **this** that I am focusing on in the beginning of my coaching model. It's good to know where you are going to, but you need a starting point, right? You need to know where you are right now, right here, today.

Otherwise, how do you know whether the journey you want to take is possible as a direct route, or whether you may need to take detours or stopovers at other places first? How will you know the distance you need to travel if you can't pinpoint your exact current location?

Self-reflection is Key

Self-reflection has been one thing that I know I have been guilty of neglecting in the past. It is often the thing we feel we need to do when we have more time, when the immediate chaos and priorities are dealt with.

Although, in reality, time creeps by and we just get **more** chaos and priorities. More things on our endless to-do lists in everyday life. I've slowly started to dislike writing myself lists of tasks that I need to do, mostly because I feel disheartened when I cannot tick them all off as complete. Not to mention the tasks that are ongoing and feature on the same spot on my list of jobs I need to do, week after week.

I realise this makes me sound a little unproductive – that's not the case, but I was starting to get to a place where I felt that anything that wasn't finished should stay on that list until it has earned its 'completed badge'. I have learned that some jobs take months, many stages, lots of iterations and in fact are never complete, but just evolving and ever-changing. Therefore, including them on a to-do list is both frivolous and makes me feel like I'm underachieving. No lists, no more! I now have a list-free mind and that feels fantastic! It is amazing what one small adjustment like that can do for your positive mind talk.

According to Life Coach Hub, we have approximately 60,000 thoughts pass through our minds every single day and 57,000 of these are habitual, meaning they are routine, common pattern thoughts and regular habit. What's more, 45,000 of these thoughts are negative.

When I read this, I was taken aback. Most of these are negative 'what ifs'. The dialogue of our self-limiting beliefs and imposter syndrome, and the voice that talks us out of trying new things, taking the leap of faith, being brave, hopeful, or wishing for something better.

It makes me think of all the times where we hear ourselves say, 'What if I fail?', 'What if I'm no good at it?'

But how about we start thinking more like, 'What if I succeed?' 'What if I am brilliant?' or 'What's stopping me?'

It makes you wonder, doesn't it? Maybe, just maybe, there's something in this. Maybe if we have more faith in our own potential, the explored and the unexplored, what could the art of the possible have in store for us?

I'm reminded of a quote that was shared with me at the beginning of my own career journey, 'Everyone dreams, why not make them true?'

My Own Little Epiphany

I have been incredibly fortunate to have magnificent experiences where my own excellent coach has helped to open my inner trail of thought, when juggling all the 'stuff', firefighting, reacting and getting my head down just to get the daily jobs and tasks completed. Historically, the to-do list would've always grown – it never becomes empty.

I took a moment to think on that. I was naïve to this little truth, somehow believing that if I push just a little harder, work a little longer, squeeze in a few more emails and restrict out any 'thinking time' for 'doing time,' then this would mean I'm working smarter, getting more done, enabling me to get involved in more projects and just doing more and more – right? **Wrong**! The more I got closer to my projects, the more I became clouded by them. I know that perspective is a wonderful tool which allows for new vision and scope, so why wasn't I prioritising this?

Taking time to think and reflect somehow seemed selfish, impractical, or just not necessary. I knew what I needed to do, the jobs that needed to be done and how I was going to do them. Stopping to start thinking was never going to tick off these actions on my list.

However – here comes the powerful part about self-reflection and, in particular for me, the link with burnout. I'm sure you might already be familiar with some of the notable signs of burnout – tiredness, persistent yawning, fatigue, low levels of concentration, headaches etc. Well, I was getting these, my body was starting to tell me that this way of working was not sustainable. It was on one particular evening that my Dad had dropped by and, being the insightful man of wisdom with a few words, just looked at me and told me in his calm Gloucestershire accent, 'You're burning out, my girl.'

How right he was! In a few short moments and by glancing at my face briefly, he was able to sum up exactly how I was feeling. He knew it before I did. I suppose I can attribute his keen eye for detail down to the fact he is a retired Detective Sergeant, or just that he is my Dad and parents have an art of seeing and knowing you better than you know yourself at times!

In a similar 1-2-1 with my line manager, I had mentioned in passing that I was feeling a little tired and she again encouraged that we discuss self-reflection and ways in which I could be incorporating this more into my working practice, but also to aid me with my own self-development.

It occurred to me that somewhere along this journey, I was stalling. Yes, I was doing my work, progressing with projects etc, but professionally I was coming to a standstill. In our discussion I found myself giving reasons and excuses why I hadn't had the time, energy or desire to spend time thinking about my own direction in all of this.

Being reminded of my core strengths, what I bring to the team and what makes me uniquely 'me', was something that came out of this conversation. Was there something in it? Could it be that spending more time focusing on me would unlock a smarter and more productive way of working, which would allow me to feel more energised? The answer was yes!

Techniques I Tried

Strengthscope®

I decided to spend time reflecting firstly on my strengths. A couple of years ago, I completed my own Strengthscope® profile, so I am aware of what my work-related strengths are.

You may have heard of Strengthscope®. If you haven't, you can find out more information at www.strengthscope.com. It is a fabulous tool with the following mission statement:

> *To reveal the unique strengths of people across the world, enabling them to bring their most authentic and inspired selves to work and to life every day.*

Strengthscope® focuses on your energising strengths. So, less about the development areas that you think you need to work on, or strengths where you are highly skilled but they simply do not energise you. Instead, the spotlight is on those strengths you have that excite you when you are using and stretching them, giving you a sense of fulfilment, value and achievement. When put this way, why wouldn't you want to do more of what you love?

When you set up your own Strengthscope® profile, you also invite your colleagues, peers and managers to rate you on these strengths. The outcome is you receive a report outlining your seven energising strengths. Your profile helps you understand where you need to be mindful when your strengths go into 'overdrive', and where you might leverage one particular strength to help you balance the lack of another.

This process helped me understand the 'me at work' and why I found some tasks and projects more exciting or engaging than others. I like to believe I was quite a self-aware person anyway, but this exercise certainly helped me identify when and where I was drawing upon certain strengths. It was no surprise for me that creativity, developing others, empathy, leadership, optimism, strategic mindedness and enthusiasm were my top seven.

I recommend using some form of 360° feedback profiling tool to help you uncover your strengths in the workplace. You might be surprised, or it might just reaffirm most of what you already know, but with the additional guidance on how you might navigate the challenges you face. This was the most powerful realisation for me. For example, my creativity being a top strength sounded about right, but in the extreme it allows me to delay, keep thinking of new ideas and exploring options, rather than committing to one and seeing it through to the end!

Myers-Briggs Personality Profile

If you haven't seen or heard of this, it is another great tool I reflect upon in my working life, whether meeting someone new, building a new coaching relationship, leading projects, managing expectations, or learning a new skill.

www.mbtionline.com

This profiles your personality, so it is more about your behaviour, how you perceive and view the world, other people, relationships with others, communication and learning style etc.

Once you understand your profile, you can't help but spot similarities and synchronies with other people, realising that they perhaps share some of your profile traits. It's also easy to spot the opposing personality trait profile types, but the detail in the descriptions allows you to understand where challenges and conflict could occur, so you can adapt your style to the situation.

Extrovert, Intuitive, Feeling and Perceiving is my profile summary.

Learning this helped me understand where, at times, I need to dial down my 'me-ness'. If you can imagine at the far extreme reaches of my personality there's a highly creative, enthusiastic, optimistic extrovert… like Tigger on caffeine! (I now understand why a previous line manager of mine kindly asked me to refrain from having both coffee and chocolate in the same afternoon!)

For fellow creatives or extroverts, this might sound like a fantastic combination, but for those more thoughtful, introverted and analytical people, it can sound like a complete whirlwind headache nightmare!

Of course, I am talking extremes here. As I mentioned, I do possess self-awareness and fortunately my strengths in empathy and intuition help me connect and understand the needs of others. So, you can see how I leverage these depending on the situation, client or circumstance.

How These Aided My Self-reflection

I began scoping out where I would next like to take each of my current work projects, using my strengths.

This activity took place on a Sunday afternoon when I was home alone in peaceful surroundings, with the sun shining and no interruptions. I decided that if I was going to fully immerse myself within self-reflection then I wanted to create a free environment and a creative space (seeing as creativity features highly on my strengths). Coloured pens, a big sheet of paper, radio music, a big glass of water (for hydration) and a scented candle, I wanted to satisfy as many senses as possible all at once. It was an experience of exploration. This is what I needed to obtain that peripheral vision, seeing beyond what was already there.

I noticed that this mindfulness activity was not only cathartic, but also energising at the same time. This was because I was approaching it with appreciation, respect and some self-love. I was subconsciously telling myself that I am important; my direction, my progression, my journey and my approach were all important.

I almost felt like a small part of my brain let out a sigh of relief as I explored on paper all the things I was aware of (and some things I was perhaps not immediately aware of), as I branched out further on what I was passionate about developing more of.

I had in mind some positive affirmations that became mantras for me:

~ Enjoy the magic of new beginnings – make that magic happen.
~ I am a walking, talking miracle magnet.
~ I attract all that I desire.

About an hour or so went by and my big sheet of paper was now full of colour, imagery, words and project brainstorming. There was extra emphasis on the big strengths and talents. These were key and where I found my energy. It's where I plug myself into the mains and create great things, instead of just topping up minimally and running on fumes!

This experience really got me thinking, pausing and considering what I wanted to work on in the future and how I wanted to work on it. It wasn't just the immediate future either, it was also the long-term. This was such an important and profound experience. I was surprised that whilst I already had all these ideas, deep down, I know I wouldn't have been able to unearth them without making dedicated time and space to really think.

I mentioned previously that my line manager was someone who fully embraced and encouraged creative thinking, so I shared my brainstorm visualisation with her. I have to say that our next coaching 1-2-1 had me brimming with excitement, enthusiasm and potential. I was back!

Preparing for Self-reflection

~ Time
~ Environment
~ The 'how'
~ Tools needed.

To prepare for self-reflection, you need to consider when you are most energised. When are you at your best?

Consider the time of day and what needs to happen before this period. Are you more energised after exercise or food?

Then think about the environment. Do you need to be outdoors, at home in quietness, or be accompanied by music or the playing of your favourite movie in the background? There's no right way with this, there's just a right way for you.

Are you motivated by fresh air, smells or textures (like a big fluffy blanket)? Or, are you at your most thoughtful after a bath? (Actually, I have many creative epiphanies in the bath!)

The 'how' is also personal to you. You might like writing things out, drawing, mind mapping, mood boarding, doing a collage, using sticky notes all over a wall, or typing frantically in a Word document. It is important you process and throw on the table all the thoughts and musings in your mind and create the setting of your choosing. There's something about a big blank piece of paper and coloured pens for me, which allows my mind to channel directly through my hands and get completely lost in the moment.

My recommendation is that you think about all these first and **then** commit to the time you are going to do this self-reflection activity. This period of self-reflection is **very important**, so try to avoid bringing in the opinions of others (even though I'm sure they are well placed and trusted). It is important you see your reflections yourself, as they link with how **you** feel.

For example, how useful is it to be told you are great at technical detail when you're more energised by developing people?

Make time in your diary, whether it's your professional or personal one. Then make it a regular feature. OK, so you might not need to expand and map out everything each time you make space for self-reflection or 'focus time', but it's a great habit to introduce. Give yourself permission to pause, get into a different headspace, nurture, play to your strengths and consider how else you may wish to take your project or work task and apply rejuvenated energy.

Self-reflection Activities You Might Try

- ~ Take a walk in nature
- ~ Meditate
- ~ Free writing – a journal or diary
- ~ Talk to yourself out loud
- ~ Try out different breathing exercises
- ~ Read
- ~ Take a bath (a personal favourite of mine)
- ~ Identify the important questions
- ~ Get creative: paint, draw, cook, bake or play music.

All these activities help you get out of the immediate fog and into a new frequency – getting out of the moment to reflect on your next steps. It's all about perspective in the moment and identifying the emotions you are feeling, as well as the task or problem. You will start to see how to separate the two and see a different view with fresh eyes. You'll be able to reflect on your current course of action. How might this be different now that you have taken a pause from that trail of thought?

Go and absorb yourself in a different experience, then come back and challenge your thoughts!

Am I Now in a State of Readiness?

It might seem strange to ask this question here, but it's a very valuable one. This question probes what you are going to do next, given this new-found inspiration you have uncovered.

It's worth checking and understanding whether now is the right time. If you are finding there are reasons that prevent you from focusing on future goals or aspirations, then maybe this is you telling yourself that you're not quite ready yet. Although, my challenge around this will always be, is there ever a perfect time?

Being in a state of readiness means you are willing and accepting that you are about to explore more, challenge yourself more, and subsequently realise that there will be things you will need to do, take ownership of, proactively research, dedicate time to, and essentially identify obstacles and transform them into new opportunities for growth.

In short, self-reflection is the tiny spark that ignites the flame. To keep the fire in your belly burning, you'll need to connect with your motivators and drivers, **and** determine a goal you are working towards.

You will also need to deeply connect with the meaning of that goal – why it is important to you, what it will mean to you to get there, what it feels like etc. It's completely fine to be unsure about what that goal is specifically, but the purpose of any coaching is to move towards something. You will become clearer on your own personal goal as we work through the stages of the coaching model, but for now, you need to really think about whether you are ready for change!

Change is both exciting and scary. Embrace both emotions – they will help you with your motivation.

Signs If You Are Not Yet Ready

You might be reading this and starting to feel a little uncertain as to whether this is really for you, or at least if you are ready right now. Consider the below checklist. If you aren't feeling that you resonate with these statements wholeheartedly, then you might want to pause and reassess when you want to make that first step.

It's bold, it's brave and it can feel unfamiliar. When you are ready, I'm right here with you.

Check-in Checklist — Are You Ready?

- ☐ I'm feeling happy, excited and curious.

- ☐ I'm open to trying new methods.

- ☐ I'm not judging myself on artistic merit – I'm simply going to have fun exploring.

- ☐ I want to create my destination goal with purpose and passion.

- ☐ I'm ready to set myself stretching action steps and am committed to following these through.

- ☐ My time is now!

- ☐ I know I hold the power to drive my own career.

- ☐ I will now begin to practise positive mind talk and give myself the following mantra:

Recite your own personal affirmation or mantra
here and say or read it to yourself every day.

Chapter Reflections

Coaching can have a fantastic impact on any individual. I have seen it from my own experience as both a coach and a coachee. Finding yourself at a career crossroads is a common place to be. We all have desires, ambitions and dreams, even if we cannot always make out exactly what they look like.

Coaching is an enabler that helps us gain clarity to unlock our inner wisdom and is our inner guide that drives us on a purposeful path.

It can sometimes be difficult to articulate exactly what we mean. We may stumble over words or find the right ones lost in that dense brain fog that we have in our mind. We know there's something there but can't quite make out the shadows and bring the conversation to the fullest.

We even have a complete mind blank, where all words and thoughts simply drain from us through the brain plughole of knowing. Trying to have meaningful coaching conversations when either of these scenarios occur (fog or empty space) can feel like a challenge and pressure that we somehow must find an answer for – any answer to the relevant question we have been asked.

This is why in this book I will talk a lot about the emphasis of your strengths, talents and passions. We won't start with the end in sight, we will start with the present, the now, and who you ultimately are.

There will be opportunities for self-reflection and time to question yourself and think a little longer about a particular thought, feeling or challenge. This isn't a process to be rushed, but one to enjoy when you are feeling like you want to work from a place of being and feeling at your best, and how to achieve **more** of your best!

Be ready to be curious, experimental, exploratory and creative. Have fun with it, be free, expand in the space where there are no limits or restrictions, and allow your imagination to flow to the art of all the possible.

Here is where the magic happens!

Chapter 2
The TARGET Model

Where It Came From

Early on whilst studying for my coaching qualification, I was intrigued by techniques and coaching models that already existed to enable powerful and rich coaching conversations. Visual techniques featured here and there (I am a big fan of image cards and other visual cues), but I was yet to come across any arty or illustrated method of coaching.

The more I began learning about the fundamental theories behind coaching, the more my go-to method of processing new learnings into visual expressions was used. Book abstracts turned into illustrated word clouds and narrative storytelling design sheets. This is how I learned how to better self-reflect, so it was also useful for playing back the key learnings and take aways I was getting from new learning experiences.

It was in a conversation with my coach, in which I was sharing these illustrations and adding them to my evidence log, when I was asked how I could use these more in coaching conversations. What if my coaching clients are also visual thinkers? How could I help other people unlock some of their 'stuck' thoughts in a visual way?

We also talked about coaching models I had started using with my clients, and reflected on the impact of these. This is when my coach asked if I had thought about using or making my own coaching model. Intriguing! Was I allowed to do this? What elements was I drawn to in other coaching models?

Influences

- ~ Instant Pay-off Coaching – Max Landsberg
- ~ GROW Model – Sir John Whitmore.

Instant Pay-off Coaching — Max Landsberg (from The Tao of Coaching book)

I really liked this model as a 'finding the root cause' tool. It reminded me a little of the Ishikawa herringbone diagram* I had learned about when attaining my Lean Six Sigma Green Belt accreditation. This technique identifies root cause and effect to introduce process improvement methods into business.

*If you're interested in learning more about this, here's a fabulous resource that explains the process (www.mindtools.com)

In the Instant Pay-off Coaching model, the key focus is centred on what the perceived 'blockers' are within a particular goal.

It's both the reality of the current situation (what stops you right now from being where you want to be?) and the process of understanding these blockers and seeing them as challenges. Or, better still, detecting the root cause for why these challenges are present, and how they could be overcome.

I've used the herringbone diagram of process improvement many times when identifying all known root causes to problems. Then, I flip it around into what all the solutions could be. You go into a place of considering all the possible opportunities and then whittle them down into most impactful, high priority, and those that represent a big return etc.

Instant Pay-off Coaching promotes similar thinking, and the challenges identified are broken down by type. I had worked on a couple of versions of this concept, both with a team in a problem-solving challenge and a coachee who had identified several obstacles that stood before them and their aspirational career goal.

It was great to see this come to life, visually, on both occasions, using visual prompts to discuss and identify solutions.

GROW Model – Sir John Whitmore

The GROW model was the one we started to reference a lot within my qualification, and indeed in the organisation I had worked for. **G**oal, **R**eality, **O**pportunity and **W**ill.

This has since become an incredibly popular and most identified coaching model for problem-solving, goal-setting and performance improvement.

I really enjoyed practising this model and connected with it more as I began to create my own visuals to represent the conversations surrounding these four stages.

I started to consider how this process could lend itself to being motivational and inspirational artwork.

I found a connection when I started converting new learnings and models with illustrations or artistic interpretations.

For the same reasons, I have always been a fan of a mood board. Something has always stuck with me when it comes to manifesting goals and the power of visual aids; a rather spiritual sense, which reminds me of the story of Jim Carrey and his road to stardom. Jim puts it down to the Law of Attraction, but in essence, this is the story...

Inspiration

Carrey Achieved the Success He Visualised

I love the story behind actor Jim Carrey's fame. Essentially, he used his motivation in his early career to attract success and find Hollywood fame. He is known to have said how he would visualise having directors interested in him, people he admired and respected appreciating his work, and opportunities he wanted being made possible for him. This was during a period where he had nothing. This mindset and focus helped him to feel better about his future prospects. Whilst they were not yet in his reality, the opportunity was out there, he just needed to attract it onto his pathway.

Even more curious, yet inspiring, he wrote himself a cheque for $10 million for 'acting services rendered' and gave himself approximately five years. He future-dated it to Thanksgiving 1995 and put it in his wallet, keeping it there all that time. It was just before Thanksgiving 1995 that he found out he was going to make $10 million on the movie, Dumb and Dumber.

(Taken from Showbiz Cheat Sheet, Published November 2020.)

Jim Carrey created a visual representation of what he wanted to manifest into his life... **and it happened**!

So, what happens if we create a visual?

We create the idea as a tangible thing.

If we bring it into being, then it's a reality.

The more I thought about this, the more I wondered if I could create a coaching model that enabled clients to create something both in the current moment and as a journey of hope, inspiration and motivation.

What if **that** was an actual thing? Imagine if I could help encourage my clients to create something and bring it into a visual existence, which in turn attracts the physical realisation and manifestation! **Wow**!

Creating Something New

Whilst I liked these coaching models and could clearly see the benefit of them in coaching practice, I wanted to stretch a little further and consider what else I needed to incorporate in my practice to create a complete creative coaching model. I wanted to create a fully immersive experience.

I gave this matter some thought and, of course, went fully into an exploratory space. What would the process look like? What did it need to include? What am I looking to achieve?

My imposter syndrome was still present, albeit a small voice in the back of my mind. Could I really create a coaching model of my own? Am I qualified enough to do so? Am I talented enough to create a model that is as effective for my clients as GROW or Instant Pay-off Coaching - both of which I was already using?

Drawing on my strengths, optimism, creativity and enthusiasm, plus my intuition, it felt right to explore this further. OK, let's go!

The Important Inclusions

A self-evaluation tool and an action plan – these are what carry the momentum, enable reflection and deeper understanding. I wanted to create something where the client had a 'take away', a call to action and something that they could use in conversation about their professional development.

I also wanted to start with some fundamental understanding of strengths and 'who I am' before going straight to the goal focus. After all, I could see that this knowledge had really helped me to get a handle of what I wanted, and the direction I wanted to travel. Maybe I should role model my own model? There's nothing to lose!

I recognised the brilliance of unpacking all the challenges in detail. Root causing and having the client identify their own solutions was incredibly powerful. I'm remembering the words of Michael Bungay Stanier in his book, *The Coaching Habit*. Staying curious for longer and not offering advice and solutions. New habits stand if they come from the individual. As such, there must be a section where the client creates the solutions for themselves.

It felt to me that the coaching conversations were incredibly powerful, but to get that rich conversation, where thoughts, expression and feeling can be articulated in a space of free-flowing creativity and openness, I wanted to give all my clients this wonderful safe space that I had found when I explored visually my own journey.

It was like finding a peaceful, untouched wilderness that isn't known to the crowds, isn't explored as a popular hotspot, but nevertheless is something impressive and special that you still want to share, to enjoy the serenity. I found this magic for myself and wondered whether it could be created for others.

Only one way to find out – and for that I needed to create a full model. One that had all the components I knew were important factors in coaching conversations and created the environment for more exploratory thinking to cultivate.

Equally, as I was also at an early stage within my own journey to discovery, I wanted to create something I could use myself. After all, I did commit to testing and role modelling it myself first.

So, my model is '**TARGET**'.

Talent, **A**im, **R**eality, **G**rowth, **E**valuation and **T**imeline.

These six stages are linked and can be worked through as a running storyline, each of them with a creative visual element that complements the questions and thinking.

T Talent: Your own Tree of Strength

A Aim: Mapping your aspirational goal

R Reality: Where are you right now?

G Growth: Turning obstacles into opportunities

E Evaluation: Taking a moment to reflect on this new perspective

T Timeline: The mini milestones that shape the next part of your journey.

You will work your way through each of these six steps and with each one have the opportunity to put pen to paper and reflect more deeply on how you feel, what you want, what you feel restricted by, and what excites you.

A Bit About Each Section

T is for Talent

I've said that I didn't want to start off by focusing on the end goal and that is very true. My coaching model kicks off with an activity I like to refer to as 'the Tree of Strength'.

This is an artistic exploration of what you resemble as an individual. All of your talents, energising strengths, aspirations, motivations, skills, values and passions. The essence of what is most important to you and what you want to take with you on the expedition towards your aspirational goal.

Connecting with what is important to you right now, and where you hold value, will help you for the rest of the journey.

Activity

In this important first step, you will be creating a strong, magnificent tree. This is a symbol of grounding, stability, resilience and growth. You will be considering what your core strengths are when creating your tree.

A is for Aim

Once you're clear on your starting point and all the valuable assets that you possess, you can begin to ring-fence the skills and strengths that you want to develop, and stretch yourself even further.

It is here where you will start to shape what your aim could look like. I use the image of a mountain to represent this, with its summit being the ultimate destination goal.

You may decide you have a couple of goals that you want to drive towards, which is fine, but it is important you give each one your full focus in turn. In other words, don't try and scatter yourself to do a bit of everything. Rather, do one excellently before turning your attention to the other.

I will get you to connect with what it feels like when achieving this goal – how it changes your life, why it's so important to you etc. Resonating with the emotions and motivators is the powerful driving force which enables you to steer with confidence.

Activity

This is where you will visualise your goal in the form of a mountain in the distance. Something that you can clearly see, but not necessarily have the precise journey mapped out.

Whilst creating your mountain, you will be channelling the energy and feelings of what it would feel like to have reached the summit of your goal. How it will change your life, what keeps you motivated and, also, why now?

R is for Reality

After being present in all that you can imagine in the wonderful space that 'Aim' encourages, you will then turn to look at where you are in the present moment. How far away are you from the goal and what potential challenges or blockers stand before you? I use the visual of a heavy wall of boulders, which you will enjoy breaking down, before moving onto the next stage.

In this section, you will also spend time identifying what these blockers are, what they represent, and how you might overcome them by beginning to consider options and solutions.

Activity

This is where you will create a boulder wall, immediately in front of you. It should be enough to prevent your pathway from being obvious, but this wall is not so cumbersome that you cannot climb over it, move bricks away, or find your way to overcome this obstacle. This represents what you imagine blocks your pathway. You also get to 'smash' and break down some of these boulders, making them smaller and more manageable. The realisation here is often that what we perceive is often not as difficult as the reality.

G is for Growth

Once you have pinpointed the challenges and possible solutions you might want to take, you will start to consider the order in which you might go about overcoming these obstacles.

The visual representation I use here is laying out a pathway to overcome the uneven terrain (using the broken-down boulders from our blocker wall).

As you begin to lay down your pathway, you will identify some easy steps to take, and which ones will take longer. Ordering them allows you to place some control over what you do, when you do it and how.

Activity

This is where you will create a pathway now that you are overcoming some of the wall blocks. You find a clearing into the fields and begin to shape your journey and understand what actions you now need to take to move forward. You can now add more colour into your image, perhaps adding in more paths, a lake, flowers, animals etc.

E is for Evaluation

This is the part where self-reflection returns and you assess all that you have understood and learned from these activities so far; looking back at the journey you've travelled to date, but also considering the rest of the journey ahead. You will check in and see whether your original goal destination is still the one in focus, or whether you have now sidetracked and wish to detour.

I will get you to look back and look forward to confirm and cement your choices and direction of travel, much like photographs of the scenery both behind and in front of you.

Activity

This is where you imagine yourself as part way through your journey. Maybe you see yourself now at your lake or at the foothills of the mountain you have created?

Here, you pause to take stock of what you have accomplished, the journey already travelled, and what else remains.

I like to use the idea of imagining photographs in this section. What signifies the path you have already travelled? What does the view now look like to you?

You might decide to paint a bridge or a boat here.

T is for Timeline

You will, by now, have a list of things you want to do or achieve (or some stepping stones) aligned to your focus goal. It is here where you start creating an action plan or a map towards the rest of your climb. You might visualise this with marker points up towards your mountain top, or a pathway of steps as you continue to climb.

This stage is your call to action. It's where you drive the changes ahead of you and make that commitment to your own development and continue to see it through.

This stage can be both your motivator and your to-do list!

Activity

You can now choose your final pathway to reaching that end goal. This could be steps to the top, or a bridge over the lake.

Mapping out your final path helps you determine some form of timeline of stages that you need to work through, knowing that you are so much closer now to reaching your goal.

You might indicate this in your bigger picture as a gestured path, but you will also create separately a very clear timeline.

The TARGET Model in Practice

I have used this model now with clients as well as on myself. I'm fascinated by the different interpretations and outcomes I see each time I work with someone new. The ease that visual working seems to offer means my clients can offload all that is in their head, all the 'and what else' content, or, as one of my clients called it, a 'visual brain vomit' of what was occupying their mind when they thought about their direction and career.

My clients felt a huge sense of cathartic freedom, exploring on paper whatever was occupying their mind, both consciously and subconsciously.

Each element they create, the choice of colour used, textures they apply or words they scribe. One thing at a time – all of which are rich conversation starting points. I welcome my clients into a supportive, vulnerable, trusted and open space. I am guided by what they feel they want to direct the conversation to first.

For me as the coach, at each stage of the TARGET model, I can see where the client begins to sense clarity, control, ideas and energy shift. It is like handing them the camera and they are choosing the lens and direction in which they wish to focus.

That 'visual brain vomit' over the sessions transforms into something meaningful, workable and encouraging for the client, transitioning into action steps that tell a story as we move towards the end of the model.

The beauty with visuals is that they can be completely abstract, meaningless to anyone else but the client. It doesn't need to make sense to the outside world; it doesn't need to have a name or a label. It's merely an extension of thought. The images created can represent anything at all. A colour, a shape, a word, a feeling, a person, a scenario, a worry, money, family, passions.

So many times I've experienced clouded brain fog, and found it difficult to pinpoint, articulate or describe to someone else why that could be. The subconscious mind dropping cryptic clues that, quite often, doesn't offer me a solution. It doesn't offer a solution because it can't – I haven't properly identified the source. It seems obvious when I break it down like this, right?

So, when I do take myself back to free expression and allow imagination of possibility to step forward, I remove all barriers, all self-limiting beliefs, doubt and judgement.

Much like with a dream, I accept it for what it is, in all the seeming bizarreness that could unfold before me. And much like with some dreams, it can hold hidden meaning or bring your awareness to something that perhaps you might need to pay attention to.

Wouldn't it be great if this whole creative thinking process could tell a story in itself?

And so, the TARGET model is born.

BONUS — It's a Work of Art

The novelty of this technique is that you are also creating, drawing and illustrating your own journey, section by section. You are building the components for your big picture, your masterpiece.

Visual thinkers (or explorers, as I often like to think of them) like to be able to see something in pictures which motivates and inspires them. It could be a method of processing new learning, or a gateway of connecting with something they hold deeper.

When working through each section of the TARGET model you are creating a visual representation of that stage of your journey. What you will have at the end is all the components that can represent an expedition or landscape adventure.

The image below is an indicator of the kind of landscape you could potentially create, and how all the elements make up the whole picture.

In my TARGET model example, it's represented by an image or series of illustrations to show 'the bigger picture'.

Each section represents a component of the journey. The strength and grounding of the tree in the foreground, the mountains of aspiration and goals in the distance, and all the mid-section pathways, fields, lake and brick walls.

I would recommend focusing on each section in turn to begin with, to work your way through the process. At the end, if you feel inspired to bring it all together in one beautiful masterpiece, then go for it! (There's more on this in the last chapter.)

You can choose how you want to represent your journey through the TARGET coaching model.

I have seen this work very well as a storyboard, with each of the stages and the images they inspire set out in a series. Through this, you can see your story unfold.

However you choose to do this, just go with it, enjoy it and be free. Explore and have fun!

It's exciting to think about how you might interpret this process, what you will learn and discover, and what you will have created by the end.

What to Expect

The TARGET model offers an alternative to coaching and self-coaching, encouraging visual thinking and using art-inspired techniques to recognise your own strengths and values, which in turn supports and drives the aspirational goal.

Using this solution-focused approach, you will be able to acknowledge any challenges and begin to view these as opportunities that support your intentions and desires.

At the time of model completion, you will have spent critical time self-reflecting and building your action plan for your next steps. Here is where all your ideas become a formalised plan of action for you to take the lead and steer towards your destination.

Coaching being channelled through this method allows for a deeper focus, reflection and opportunity to gain greater clarity as you explore with freedom all the subconscious and conscious ideas in your awareness.

If you previously found you were one of those people who experiences a 'brain freeze moment', or can't quite navigate through your own mind fog, the TARGET model will help you make sense of that and enable you to become clearer on your future direction.

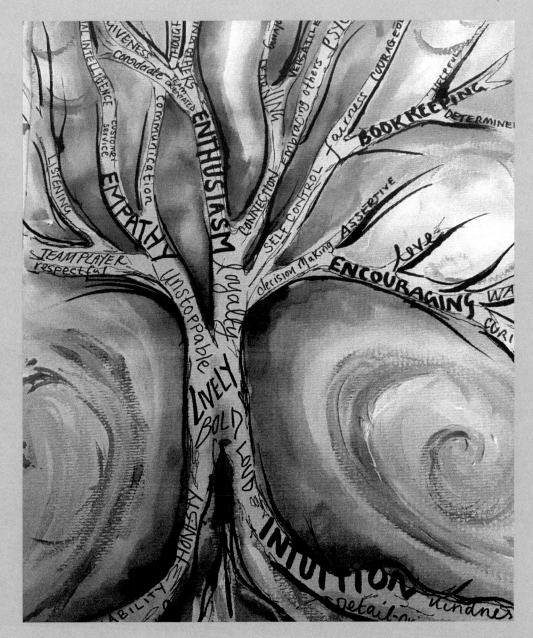

Chapter 3
T = Talent:

Your Own Tree of Strength

Why We Should Focus on Our Strengths

I've mentioned profiling tools such as Strengthscope® which are powerful and motivating because they enable us to focus on our strengths and not our weaknesses. It makes more sense when you come to think of it really, doesn't it?

An Olympic diver does not spend their time focusing on their speed in which they complete the length of the pool; they focus on their diving technique as this is their strength and talent, and they want to get **even better** at it. It is much the same with the long-distance runner. He/she doesn't berate themself for their time out of the starting block, they invest in their endurance performance as this is their strength.

There are many other examples, I am sure, of where top athletes, public speakers and many professionals focus on their talents over their development areas, to just become even more brilliant. This is also because it's motivational and it feels good to be great at what they love. We all should be doing more of what we love, right?

So, here I will be asking you to focus on your strengths too. To consider all the things you know you are great at, that you enjoy, where you get a sense of value, purpose and pride. Include within this your talents and skills, whether natural or learned, where you excel, where you achieve and where you are driven and motivated. Imagine if you had a role where you were **doing more** of these things and **feeling more** energised because you were performing from a place of passion.

Working at OUR BEST

I hear this a lot within organisations, bringing your best self to work. I genuinely love this concept. I was lucky, as I mentioned earlier, that I have had line managers who wanted to nurture this within me. It truly is such a feeling of value and appreciation when you are encouraged to bring the best version of yourself to your place of work. What I mean by this is that it's someone really taking the time to understand you, what ignites you and what makes you tick, to which they then try and encourage your approach to tasks and projects to play to these strengths to get the very best from you, **and for you**.

It goes without saying (but I will say it, anyway!), you are likely to give more when you are utilising strengths that link to what you love. A happier you makes you more productive at work, for example.

I have an example of where my line manager leveraged my strengths beautifully...

I was working on a major project and there were some snags which needed identifying and resolving. It wasn't obvious what the solution might be. It would need some time to investigate further.

My line manager suggested that to connect with this task and thrive, I might want to lean on my creativity and empathy strengths to do some root cause analysis.

We talked about what that could mean, but I decided on a group meeting, using visual aids, sharing screens and mapping out together. Different colours and charts highlighted all the problems we were facing together as a group, but also all the potential solutions we could investigate.

The result was that I had identified what my stakeholders recognised as being their major sticking points, and through visual solution mapping there was a clear outcome and action which was implemented the following week. This fixed the problem, but equally exercised and demonstrated my strengths and my value.

The learning for me from taking this approach is that there isn't just one way to go about any challenge. I could have adopted a method that worked well for one of my colleagues, but if I remember my strengths and choose one (or two) of these to utilise, then I am more likely to thrive whilst I perform.

Just something to think about.

Where Did the 'Tree of Strength' Come From?

I started to think about my own journey and see myself as a case study. The difficulty I had was knowing that I wanted to develop and grow, but I wasn't sure what that looked like or what I would be doing? I knew I needed to become clear on this, to set my own goal. It did make me wonder how many other people might also find themselves wondering the same thing.

I went back to my 'roots', so to speak, whenever I wanted to figure something out, understand the mind fog and allow all the scattered thoughts and ideas to have a stage and their time in the limelight. I knew I needed to move this into something visual.

Tree of Strength, this is your two-minute curtain call!

I wanted to illustrate something that was going to represent stability, grounding, roots, strength and growth, but also resilience. Being a spiritual soul and someone who often practises mindfulness techniques, I've always found a real beauty in nature and trees. It seemed fitting that for me to grow on a journey and travel in a career direction, I needed a firm starting point, and a tree represents all of this for me.

I wanted to see myself as this tree and use this visual cue as a motivator, a driver, for all that I am now and all that is important to me. I want it to represent all my strengths, skills, passions, values and talents.

I spent an hour or two on a Sunday morning mapping out all the fundamental elements of my tree. On each twisty branch I starting to pen words that detailed my traits and strengths. I wanted to focus on the energy that this exercise was giving me, recognising skills I have learned and acquired, but considering which of these gave me true energy and left me feeling inspired.

Tree of Strength, now is your time to take centre stage!

So, here we have it, my first Tree of Strength. As I intuitively sketched and added the important wording, I was acutely aware I was starting to tap into some special magic. Almost like those moments just before you fall asleep when your subconscious mind bursts in with a reminder for something you were meant to do. I figured that the subconscious mind does this when you try to quieten it too much, at least mine does! It then starts to **shout** at me to take notice, usually in vivid dreams, or burnout symptoms in my body – as I mentioned earlier.

The moments when I was free drawing and free writing, I honestly didn't feel like I needed to think hard or engage my brain too much, as the escapism of drawing took over. Maybe this is also how some people allow themselves to get totally lost in a piece of music, or far away deep in a book.

Stepping back from this, I started to then ponder some key features. I noted I had chosen autumnal colours; ironic really, as it's my least favourite season. I've always attributed it to endings, darkness setting in, with new life and beginnings so far away. But, like with plants and trees, when the blooms begin to die and the leaves start to fall, all the energy goes back beneath the surface, to grow stronger, weather the storms ahead and come back brighter and more vivid when the time is right.

Considering this metaphor, it became clearer to me that what I was doing was essentially focusing on my core. Whatever beautiful journeys bloom from this, in all the twisty branch directions, it's all based on how I nurture my own fundamentals.

I still use this Tree of Strength as my starting block, whenever I want to go back to basics and review a new route, a different path, or a new focus. I check back in with this tree, sometimes adding to it as it evolves over time. What I did following this exercise was start to be selective with what I knew I wanted to take with me into the future. For example, I love using art as a way of making sense and understanding projects and learning. I asked myself, 'Is this a strength that makes me **energised**?'

I ring-fenced all the strengths where I felt I got something back from using them – something positive, enriching and inspiring.

I know that one of my strengths is also an eye for detail, but this doesn't serve me as a massive strength that I wanted to explore doing more about. Not at this time.

Developing others and empathy were big drivers, so whatever I was going to do next needed to fill these buckets. I knew I wanted to focus on coaching others and develop my coaching practice even further.

I mapped all these wonderful and magical strengths that I loved using, which energised me. I then started to consider where or how I could develop these further. I couldn't wait to have a conversation with my own coach (at the time, this was also my line manager) to share with her what I had discovered in this self-reflective exercise.

'I think what all this points to is that I want to develop my coaching skills.' 'I want to study a coaching qualification and learn how I can bring more of **me** into coaching.'

I set myself up with a plan of what this would mean to me, why it would benefit my skill set, and avenues in which I could explore this additional learning. By now, I was giddy with excitement, as this just felt so incredibly right. Three months later I began to study my qualification. Fast-forward 12 months and I've created my own coaching model and have written this book to share it with you!

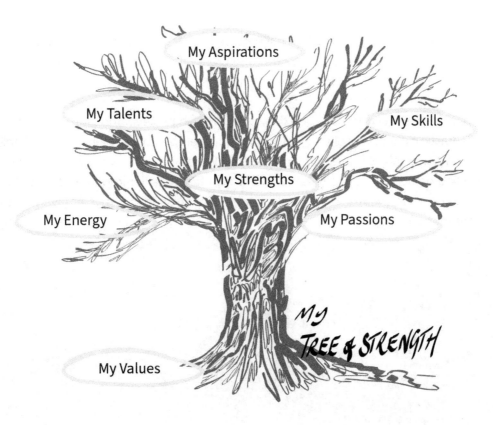

My Aspirations

My Talents

My Skills

My Strengths

My Energy

My Passions

My Values

My TREE of STRENGTH

How I've Used It Since

This is now a common feature within my coaching practice and has shown some very positive results. (Check out some of the endorsements at the end of the book if you are curious as to how it has helped my clients so far.)

I have evolved it slightly from the first version I used for myself, but all the key components are there.

When I ask my clients to think about their strengths, I encourage them to consider all the things they know they are great at, plus the things that others tell them. To explore all the passions and hobbies that are outside of work, as well as within work life. Identifying what motivates, inspires and what gives you energy, are also included on the tree.

You will see the focal headings I have placed on the illustration. I usually send this template to my clients and ask them to create their own version of the Tree of Strength.

I genuinely get excited when I see their creations. No two ever look the same. They are fantastic expressions of that individual, and I feel I get to see them in more detail through doing this exercise. Similarly, when I did this myself, I was aware of what I identified personally during the activity. I was putting heavier importance on some words and skills over others. This signified where I was telling myself I wanted to create more space to grow.

How Do You Create Your Own Tree of Strength

The Technique

Now, please don't be put off that because I love drawing and illustrating that somehow you need to create a photographic quality tree image. None of the techniques I have created depend on any artistic talent. Doodles, sketches and freehand scribblings **all** work perfectly well.

If you love using scrapbooking techniques, then sure, why not collage your tree with different papers, cut-outs from magazines, postcards or newspapers. There are literally **no rules**. Be free and explore.

What I will say before you begin this exercise, is consider when and where you want to do this. Where are you when **you** are most energised, happy and relaxed? Consider the time, environment and surroundings. I needed the house to myself, with background music and a coffee. But this is your time, so make it however you need to. Plan in the time – a self-reflective date with yourself!

Top Tips for Preparation

~ Find space – this can be a large table, the floor, or walls if you like to stand.

~ Hydrate and eat something – one less thing for you to have to think about. You don't want belly grumbles and your waking conscious overriding this magic with 'feed me now' chants!

~ Find the right time – do you need to plan ahead, making your loved ones aware of your 'focus time' to limit any interruptions, wherever possible?

~ Find your tools – paper, coloured pens, pictures, stickers, Post-it notes. Whatever tools you want to use here, choose what you are comfortable using. If you prefer to do this digitally, go for it. I prefer using my hands and freestyle, but this needs to be right for you.

~ Final environment adjustments – heating, a jumper, a window open, music on etc.

Now, you can begin!

I refer to this model as a journey and a way of creating your **big** picture. You can, of course, create each activity in this model in any way you choose, using the template elements I have included. Here, though, you will see how this all forms a 'big picture'.

Let's Get Drawing

Sketching out a tree can be simple. Here's how:

THE SIMPLE TREE

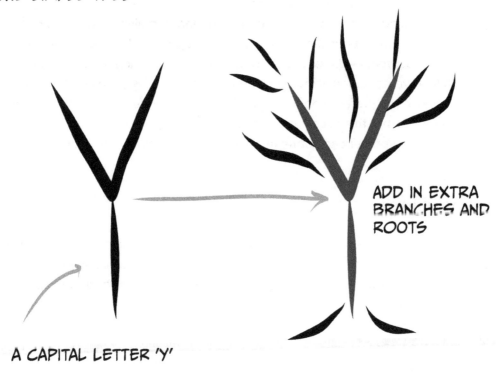

A CAPITAL LETTER 'Y'

ADD IN EXTRA BRANCHES AND ROOTS

Voila! A tree.

You can spend as much time as you would like creating leaves, colours and textures. Equally, you can use the branches to add words and indicate your strengths, talents, skills, passions, motivators and inspirations.

Freestyle

You can completely freestyle your tree and play about with different mark-making techniques. I love the contrast of using different pens and their line thickness. Here, I've just used a couple of line styles and doodled freestyle.

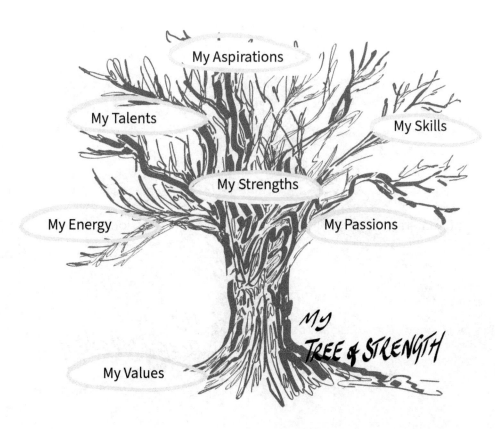

Use the illustration to help you map out and brainstorm all your strengths, skills, passions etc.

To help you identify what to put in each section, I've included some descriptors below:

~ **Aspirations** – What inspires me? Where do I want to go?
~ **Values** – What is important to me? How do I like to work?
~ **Passions** – What do I love? What do I want to do more of?
~ **Strengths** – What do I know I'm great at?

- **Talents** – Where do I excel in particular? How does this align to my personality?
- **Skills** – What qualifications or practical knowledge do I have? What have I learned and perfected?
- **Energy** – What do I do that motivates or excites me the most? How or where do I recharge?

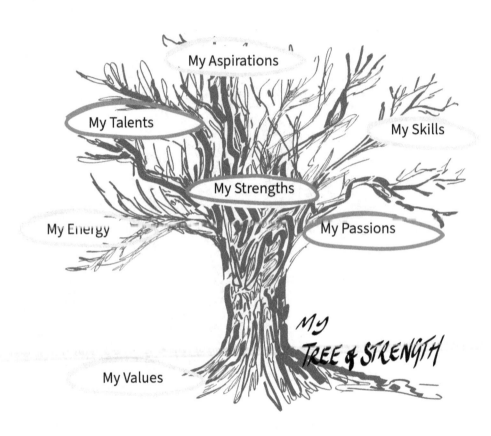

Under-utilised STRENGTHS

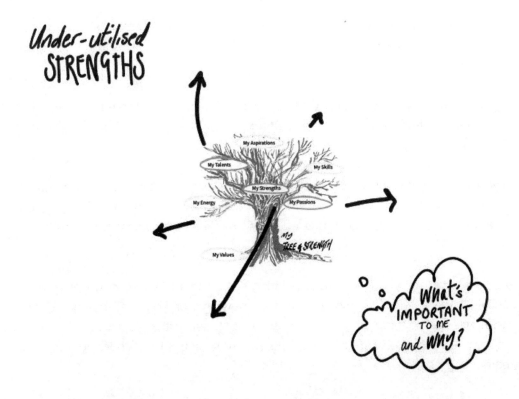

Then highlight the strengths you feel are under-utilised at present. Ones that you are not currently demonstrating at all, or at least not to their fullest. You may want to highlight using a different colour.

Now think about **why** they are under-utilised. How important are they to you?

Do you want to use these more in the future?

Think about ways you have, or could have, demonstrated these. What are the opportunities in your current role and in your personal life?

How much more time would you like to dedicate to developing these, and where? Is it at home or is it in your career?

What would your ideal next move look or feel like to you?

I invite you to get this down on paper. Creating a brainstorm or mind map can work well here – a cloud or bubble with the words 'My under-utilised strengths', or, bolder still, 'My hidden gems'!

If you prefer, you could just list these on paper. Try not to be too rigid though. Let your thoughts flow freely (you aren't putting them into a plan of action or structured format just yet).

If you are energised by pictures and images, then create a mood board. Add photos, positive affirmations, powerful words and phrases that mean something to you. Really connect with the under-utilised strengths and express how motivated these make you.

As an example, if you are great at painting or baking, recognise how doing these activities makes you feel and what impact they have on your well-being, but also acknowledge how important they are to be included within your work. It may be that you love the freedom to be creative, so it may be this that is missing from your career at present.

You have a choice to consider when reviewing your strengths. Which ones can be fulfilled by hobbies, interests and your personal life, and which ones do you feel **must** be included in your work? This helps you define your purpose and your value. To be at your very best, performing in your dream role, what skills and talents are you using?

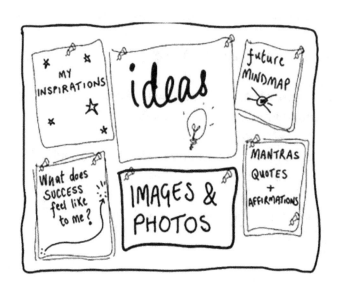

Creating a visual representation of all your strengths, and taking the time to understand those that are not currently being fulfilled, will help shape what is important to you for your future career journey.

This will help you stay motivated over challenges and be a reminder of 'why' you are doing this, what it means etc.

You may decide that now is not the right time to venture further, but when you are ready, it is here for you to pick up and take forward.

Chapter Reflections

By now, you should be clear on what those all-important strengths are and how much you value these in whatever you do. You may even be slightly impressed with your illustration and how much fun you had working in this way.

Whether you already knew your career goal or not, this exercise should have cemented fundamental criteria that you want to take with you, and develop, as you continue with your career. These skills and strengths make up who you are. Your best self, the best version of you. You may have chosen to ring-fence some attributes that have more weight and significance to you in the future. You may have identified some that you are happy to keep separate from work, which is fine.

I want you to imagine all of what could be possible. What if you had a role where you stretched and thrived using these skills and strengths all the time? Imagine how that would feel.

Interestingly, how much of these strengths do you utilise in your current role? Are there any that are under-utilised that you want to bring to the forefront?

Whenever I am working with my graduates or those clients in the early stages of their careers, I ask them not to solely focus on the job role they are aspiring for. It's not about the title or the sector, it's more about how you align your strengths into whatever you are doing. Make the most of them and decide which ones you want to empower and drive you.

You will naturally get recognised and valued when you are working from this place. The ability and talent simply radiates from you, as you're completely connected when working from your energising strengths.

Don't we all want to just do what we love and be fantastic at it?

I'm offering you this thought. How can you make it your reality?

Start thinking about where this could take you and where you would like to go with it. Your next stage of the TARGET model will be about having aim in your focus. You can think short-term and long-term here. How far do you want to reach with this? What's next for you? What does success feel like to you?

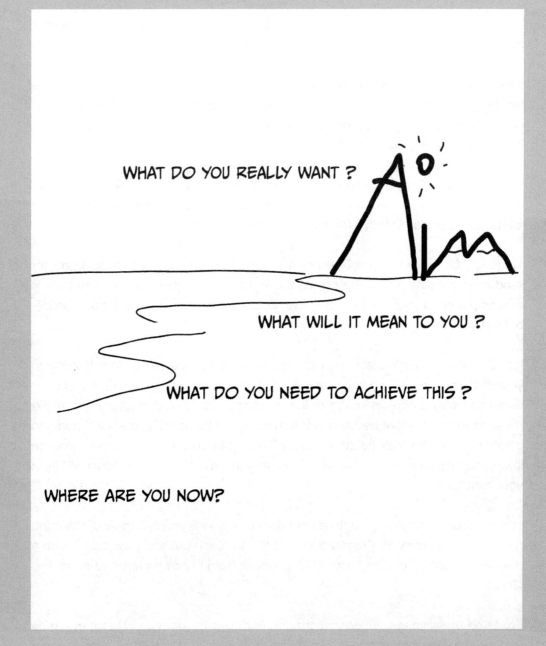

WHAT DO YOU REALLY WANT ?

WHAT WILL IT MEAN TO YOU ?

WHAT DO YOU NEED TO ACHIEVE THIS ?

WHERE ARE YOU NOW?

Chapter 4
A = Aim:
Mapping Your Aspirational Goal

You can now start considering what your goal might be. What it looks like, what it feels like, why you want to achieve it, what it really means to you.

If we had started with this at the beginning, you might have been able to articulate this fairly well, but my guess is that you, like many of my coaching clients to date, now feel better equipped, more charged and ready to explore more about what being at your very best can look like.

By creating your 'Tree of Strength', you have developed your own unique motivator tool; something you can go back to at any time and check why you are on this journey, who you are doing it for, and what your purpose is.

There will be times when you will suffer at the hands of my old friend, imposter syndrome, but your Tree of Strength is the kryptonite for when this nemesis begins to stomp around your inner psyche and recites some of those self-limiting beliefs back at you.

Use the power of the visual interpretation as a habitual focal point. Have it stuck on your wall, at your desk, photograph it as your screensaver, or create your own diary reminders with a pop-up image of it. Use strong, positive affirmations and recite these to yourself before bed and in the morning. All these techniques will begin to create positive mind talk habits, and your Tree of Strength image will, over time, be imprinted on your mind, so that when you start to think about it, you see it vividly in your mind's eye.

I think about my Tree of Strength every time I take a walk and see trees that remind me of the one I created. Wherever I can, I like to reach out and physically touch a tree, as if reconnecting and establishing power from my own identified strengths. (Try it!)

Fixate on these images when you are connecting with your goal. This is the force that will drive you and continue to motivate you. Your goal should be a heightened version of all the great energy you now feel, **and so much more**.

The power of thought is great. Let your mind take you to all the possibilities.

How You Identify the Goal

I like to think of this activity as an imaginative wish list for your life. Whatever you want exists in this life already, or at least the tools to create it or the people who can open doors, do.

It all already exists. Which means it is all possible. It's a matter of aligning, attracting and manifesting it to be a part of your life.

I'm a huge believer in the Law of Attraction. I won't go into all the detail here, but the crux of it is that we invite into our lives our thoughts and beliefs. If you programme your mind in such a way to see struggle, debt, challenge and heartache, the Law of Attraction acts as a magnet to ensure you get more of the same. In other words, your full focus and energy is geared to focus and give importance to these things, meaning you will likely attract more of the same, acknowledge you 'knew this was coming' and that 'this kind of thing always happens to me'. **Stop, just stop**!

Imagine if you started thinking from another viewpoint, something like, 'I'm learning more every day', 'my confidence and strength continue to grow' and 'I'm attracting more financial abundance into my life'. The results of this way of thinking are endless and impressive.

I won't preach to you any further, but I will share with you how I have seen this work for me, although not yet on the scale of Jim Carrey. (I'm still working on that!)

Law of Attraction – Changing Thought Patterns to Attract Results

A few years ago, I was working as a leader with a significant number of direct line reports. I enjoyed leading people, but what I loved the most was being able to support the development of others, to see them grow, transform and become successful. (I didn't know then, but this links exactly with my 'developing others' strength!)

There were parts of my role that I enjoyed, but these were becoming areas where I was beginning to feel a little flat, without zest, aloof, indifferent. I just felt OK. I wasn't disengaged, but I was beginning to feel a little unhappy – I just couldn't pinpoint why this was.

It was at this stage in my life when I met my great friend, Bitesh. A very capable, successful but humble individual who seemed to have life sussed out. He appeared to be someone who was always grateful for what he had, but what I also admired was his desire to push himself – a sort of spark for life.

It was Bitesh who introduced me to the meaning of Law of Attraction and how he used this himself. I noticed that even the terminology he used in response to me asking about his day was always strong and full of emotive words like 'awesome', 'fantastic', 'living the dream'. I used to think this odd at first, as most people I came across responded with the usual bland, 'yeah, I'm good thanks' or 'my day has been OK/fine'.

What I was learning was that mindset played a big part in his success, or what he viewed success for him to be like.

At this point, I wasn't exactly sure what I wanted to do next in my career, but I liked the idea of working within a Learning and Development team. I was aware our organisation had one, but the roles were typically based over 100 miles from where I lived. I dismissed even entertaining that thought… at that point, anyway.

I started practising more positive self-talk and considered what I wanted to attract into my life. I had conversations with people in the organisation I had previously shied away from, as I wasn't sure they would see my potential or transferable skills.

Positive mind talk, meditation and mindfulness all kickstarted my thought processes and made me bolder to try more. I created my first career mind map. It included all the things I wanted to achieve and 'want' within the next 12 months. Thinking about that Law of Attraction concept – that everything I want already exists – I could include anything in my goals.

A newer car, the salary I wanted to be earning in 12 months (I made this bold but realistic based on my experience and qualifications), the type of work I would be doing and the type of team I would be working with, all featured on my list.

I added things like the types of holiday it would enable me to pay for, for my family, and my overall sense of well-being and contentment.

The most important part of this exercise was that I created the intention and accepted that it would all fall into place in divine time.

I meditated regularly and recited my own positive affirmations, joined yoga classes, and began appreciating and feeling grateful for how I was feeling.

I had a couple of opportunities to support our Learning and Development team on projects, so I volunteered, reached out and joined in. I viewed this at the very least as giving me valuable experience, and I could decide whether I liked being a part of this, or whether it was perhaps not right for me after all.

A couple of months passed, and a vacancy came up in the team, but at a senior level.

I went through four stages of interview. At the last stage, the role was offered to someone with a little more experience who fitted the senior role more appropriately.

Now, here's where the magic happened for me! Something within me knew that this was all going to plan.

Whilst admittedly a little disheartened, I had done so much work on my own mental well-being and felt so excited and driven. Something within me knew that there was something else around the corner and I just needed to hold out and wait.

Later that week, I had another call. There was to be another vacancy, which only materialised that same week. It was more aligned to the work I had done leading others and supporting them to develop their careers. I was offered a full-time position.

I was thrilled, it offered me the opportunity to work more creatively and develop my own learning. What's more, I was joining a newly-formed team. Incidentally, the guy who was offered the senior role turned out to be a fantastic colleague, hugely talented, and I'm honoured I got to work with him. A new leader was also appointed (Emma). She had such a profound impact on my development, and still does to this day!

It was only when I reflected and stumbled across my original mind map over Christmas that year, that I realised all I had wished for had happened, and in just a few months.

My salary was exactly as I had specified. I had booked us on a couple of wonderful family holidays. I was feeling great, **and** I was able to change my car for a newer model.

I remember recollecting the series of events with a group of friends over the festive period, who were intrigued by my achievements that year, and seemingly how much I had started to 'glow'.

Simply put, the Law of Attraction came into play, because I had the belief in myself and changed my thinking habits. I was more appreciative, grateful and accepting of the fact that things work out for you at exactly the right time. When one door closes, it's to make way for another that is about to open.

If you don't get the job you wanted, something else is for you instead. That's what I took from this, and I had faith it would turn out how I had visioned.

I know that anyone can do this – as I did. The trick is to not be limited by what currently contains you. Look beyond and, of course, have a truly **awesome** day!

Framing the Focus

Hopefully you are having fun pondering your own wish list. You will soon be creating this with clarity and focus. To do so, you may need to narrow down your goals and address one at a time. New financial gains, a new job, a newer car and more holidays formed part of my mind map. You should focus on the enabler for all the things in your mind as your primary goal focus.

This will, more than likely, be a career move. It's good to have all the other things on the wish list on the periphery, as the focus at this point should be on that one goal (career). Trust me, everything else will follow in good time!

WHAT DO YOU REALLY WANT ?

WHAT WILL IT MEAN TO YOU ?

WHAT DO YOU NEED TO ACHIEVE THIS ?

WHERE ARE YOU NOW?

Aim – Having the Goal in Mind

We are now ready to explore what the actual goal looks like. I'm a big fan of visualisation techniques for interpreting what a goal may be. Your goal should always have a purpose, a calling, or a true connector to your passions and motivations; otherwise, why do it?

Connecting with your core strengths at the beginning is how I encourage you to cut out all the background noise. Yes, your friends and partner etc tell you that you would make a fantastic manager, or you should set up your own business, or that you could sell more if you did open a shop, or you should go for the promotion in accounts because you're great with data.

It's wonderful to have such encouragement and insight from those around you, but there is just one problem with it. It's not coming from you!

Remember how I said that there are strengths you have but they do not energise you? You are a fantastic and talented being, but what is important is that you work towards a goal you are 100% aligned to. After all, it is you who will be doing this; it's your happiness, your choice, your strengths.

When you have a goal in mind, one that resonates from you, ticks the boxes of strengths you wholeheartedly wish to explore, and something that you know you will love doing, learning and growing, **then** we can start working on what it all involves.

How, when and where you do this next activity are all key. Create the space, dedicate time to your own development and reflections, and begin!

The Technique

By now, there should be a lot more clarity over what you want to continue to develop – the skills and strengths you want to grow to see what further potential can be unlocked.

When I use this technique with a client, this is the time they may begin to realise the direction they wish to travel. I say to them it is a time to dismiss 'people say I should do, x, y and z', and concentrate more on what **you** are passionate about.

Hold this thought for a moment or two, and imagine what your ultimate dream career looks like.

- ~ What are you doing?
- ~ Where are you working from?
- ~ What is the environment?
- ~ What does this enable you to do more of?
- ~ How does it feel to be working in this way?
- ~ What does it really mean to you?

It is in this place of imagining that I want you to connect with all the emotions, feelings and energies, and ask you to indicate this visually. Different colours and shapes work well here and represent the important elements that surround you in this wonderful space.

I have done versions of this before with sticky notes, different coloured pebbles and hand-drawn icons. There are no rules, but if you want something specific to work with, here's a very abstract method that works very well – the trick is trying not to overthink.

Activity

- ~ Grab a big sheet of paper and choose a colour to represent your aim/goal.
- ~ Choose a colour to dedicate to that goal and draw a circle to indicate its place on the page.
- ~ Now choose another colour and consider a surrounding factor which supports this goal. Draw a circle on your page to indicate this supporting factor. It might be close to your goal or underneath it.
- ~ Use more colours, shapes and circles to symbolise other 'things' that impact on, or are a consideration towards, potentially achieving this goal. These might be steps to take or obstacles to overcome.
- ~ Don't worry about trying to figure out what each shape, colour or circle might represent straight away. Be intuitive.
- ~ Keep adding until you feel it is complete.

Reflection

I want you to now observe the following:

~ Notice the positioning of your shapes. Where are they in relation to one another? What colours are being used?
~ Are there preferred colours you have used? Are there any colours you consciously chose not to use?
~ Do you want to add any labels to your shapes?
~ What words are you using?
~ Where are **you**? If you were to choose a colour and draw a circle that indicates your place in this, where would you be? Draw yourself in where you feel you are.

Now think about or write down:

~ What does each shape represent to you?
~ Do some of these circles, shapes and colours represent people or feelings?
~ Do some of these represent challenges, experiences or situations?
~ What are all of these 'things' you have symbolised?

Two big questions you need to answer at this point:

~ What have you understood better by doing this process?
~ What areas do you need to focus on, to get to where you want to be?

Case Study –
The End Goal

One of my clients did this activity with me and they were quite clear about their end goal. They drew a symbol to represent this.

They then drew themselves in a place where they were looking upwards towards this goal, but there was so much space in-between.

Components were added into the spaces and symbols were created, which they later gave names to: knowledge, experience and confidence. These had been identified as the things that would grow and evolve as they moved closer to their goal, but were also the things that stopped them from being close to the goal at this particular moment.

As we started to focus on each element in turn, I could see the commitment and readiness to develop these attributes come forward. There was something in this experience that was visibly making them more motivated to keep momentum with their own development. When I asked them to consider what this picture would look like in six months' time, they were very clear that these symbols and objects would feature much closer to them on the page, or even form a part of them as if being worn like badges of pride; their character symbol was also spatially placed closer to the goal.

It's clear to me that the things that surround our dreams and goals are the important bridges or vehicles for us to get to the destination.

These represent part of the 'reality'; our awareness of where we are right now and what we feel is preventing us from jumping straight into that wonderful place immediately.

It's important to keep reflecting on your goal and think about where these could be present in your journey. What needs to be overcome to move you closer to where you want to be?

Once comfortable with your representation of your goal, you are ready to explore your realities in more detail, which beautifully leads us onto the next chapter.

Chapter Reflections

I hope you have enjoyed this exercise. It's quite an exploratory, future-thinking space, but if you remove the self-limiting mind talk and keep yourself centred in a place where anything could be possible, it's a powerful tool to use.

I love working with my clients and witnessing when they see this all unfold. I normally ask them to talk about what they created when they were seeing themselves living and working in the success of achieving their goal. I notice the shift in their energy, the fire in their eyes, and how they are eager to start the ball rolling.

When I ask them about the most useful element of this exercise, time and again they come back with self-reflection and focus. It allowed them to stop and think.

It's easy to get caught up in the everyday, to go with the flow and just live for the weekends and holidays. I used to do that myself, counting down to Friday and feeling like I was only allowed to enjoy and be my best self at weekends. It's bizarre, really, when you think about it. Why can't we live a life where every day we bring our best selves, work from a place of passion, talents and strengths, celebrate how that feels and what it gives back to us, and enables us to do and be completely grateful for all of it?

So, my challenge to you from now on is:

- ~ What will you do to ensure you make your goal your reality?
- ~ What thinking patterns might you change to create new habits?

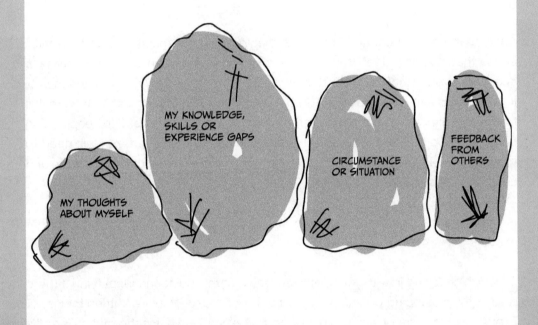

Chapter 5
R = Reality:
Where Are You Right Now?

Great work so far! Connecting with what drives you and where you want to take that next step to thrive and succeed is fantastic visionary thinking.

You can start to have both images you have created next to each other. I encourage you to keep taking photos on your phone so you have access to these wherever you are. Why not email them to yourself too!

You are beginning to create a story of your journey through images. The tree is, of course, your stability, your roots and your grounding. Your mountain is where your goal is.

Amid all the excitement and dreamlike imaginings, there might also be the realist in you that acknowledges there's so much to do in-between where you are now and where you want to be. The duration of the journey is very much down to you. If your plan is a longer-term one and the goal is more than 12 months away, that is fine, but you know you are in this for the long haul. So, you will need to keep pulling on those important strengths and drivers to keep you motivated. You will need to remind yourself why you are doing this, and you will need to learn to appreciate and celebrate the successes on the way.

Remember though, your reality, where you are right now, is all relative to your current mindset.

It's worth checking in with your own well-being at this point and identifying if there is something stopping you, holding you back, or a reason you are putting things off. Explore a little more of why this might be. For example, what is the root cause? It's from here where the hard work will start, so you want to make sure you are in that state of readiness. (You can refer back to the checklist in Chapter 1 if you need to.)

Wow... There's More to This than First Thought!

Yes, I've been there! I've had that goal in mind, I'm celebrating my skills and talents already, and I have aspirations of where these can take me in the future. But, oh my, I realise there seems to be a lot that stands in my way! Or, in other words, when I think about what stops me from being in that place of achieving my goal tomorrow, there are a lot of 'things' I need to do first, or hurdles to overcome.

Don't let this overwhelm you, though. Remember, forewarned is forearmed!

Identifying what the challenge is most certainly aids you in overcoming it. Wouldn't you rather know now and be clear about what potentially lies ahead? Surely it will give you the line of sight to be able to navigate. When you turn on the headlights when it's dark, they light up the road ahead. You may not be able to see all the path, but you will certainly begin to see what's likely coming next.

Self-doubt

I think it's probably normal to feel a little daunted. Honestly, each time I am about to embark upon something new or venture into unfamiliar territory, I am a bit scared. I'm also incredibly excited.

This is because whenever I am developing myself or stretching my skills further, I make sure it aligns with my core values, talents and strengths from my Tree of Strength. These are my allies in the uncertain space I am in. Like specialist tools you are fully equipped with for your expedition.

Yes, you might be venturing into unchartered waters or uneven terrain, but you already have all that you need to navigate this.

Feeling that little bit unnerved or scared is a good sign, it shows that it matters and that you want it… and we know it's definitely going to help us grow! If it doesn't test or stretch you, then is it worth doing? We appreciate that all the people we see as being highly successful would have had these moments. Dig deep, find your reserves, your motivators, and go for it!

Let's Face Your Reality Blockers

REALITY BLOCKERS

It's often at this stage where the challenges and blockers that stand between us and where we really want to be become clear. More often, when I have done this process with my clients, there is a pleasant surprise that these challenges turn out to be less scary and looming than their minds had previously led them to imagine.

This is what fear does – and especially fear of the unknown. Self-limiting beliefs like this space too, they like to dress up and call out our 'imposter' version of ourselves, telling us all the things that we can't do because we are not clever enough, qualified enough or talented enough. We don't have the right skills, or our situation doesn't allow this to be any more than just a dream.

When we look at each of these blockers square in the face, bravely, with recognition and give them each an identity, they start to somehow become smaller. They lose their scare factor and power over us when we can identify them (much like many fictitious demons and monsters).

What can be most scary of all, is that we create these blockers in our mind's eye with such enormity and apprehension. This is where we can completely talk ourselves out of the idea, passing it off as foolish dreaming, akin to 'only if I won the lottery, could that be possible' type of thought process.

The power of the mind is fascinating, isn't it? Yet, we are aware that these aspirations could be possible for us, right? I mean, they exist and are real for some people right now, already, today. This didn't just happen out of nowhere. At some time or another, someone had a plan, a thought, a dream and despite facing obstacles and challenges, decided they would persevere, looking for ways to overcome these obstacles, break them down or navigate a different way to achieving their goal.

Let's Take a Visualisation Journey Together

Have someone in your mind that you feel is successful, in a true peak of their career or life. They can be famous or someone you know well.

See them through your eyes, how they appear to you.

Think about the successes they may have had on the road to getting to where they are right now.

Imagine how amazing that must feel for them, living the way they do, and passionate about what they do, the mark they have made on others and how they have created such a life.

Visualise you standing beside them and feeling all the things they do, seeing and experiencing their life as they do.

Through their eyes now.

Spend a moment or two appreciating and really enjoying their life, as if it were your own.

Now, let's look a bit deeper, whilst still in this place of gratitude. Ask yourself – has it always been this easy for them?

Have they met challenge or adversity?

What obstacles or blockers might have been present for them on this journey, growing up, moving jobs, relationships, finances, health etc.

Acknowledge that somehow, in some way, they worked through these. They decided to respond and shape their own actions because their drive and desire was greater than what their perceived challenges were.

Imagine if you were able to do the same for yourself. Believe that you can!

It's the typical iceberg effect, isn't it? We only see above the surface and take that as what we know. But beneath that success is a back story. Learnings, where concepts were tried and tested but were not quite right, setbacks, challenges, upheaval, uncertainty, being refused, let down, not qualifying, relationship break-ups, death, separations, loss, redundancies, hurt, or even just experiences that simply did not go to plan for no reason whatsoever.

The truth is, we will never be able to escape these aspects of life, we know this really. We deal with challenges when we have no choice, when they are imposed upon us, or when we need to in order to survive. That's what makes us incredible and resilient human beings. If we can do this under pressure when we are pushed to do so, and overcome the challenges, work through the fear and become stronger for it, why can we not see challenges or blockers that stand before a path that we **choose** to travel, with open eyes, and see this as an opportunity to grow, instead of a reason to give up?

The Technique

Let's take this visualisation onto paper and create what these blockers look like and represent for you. What is stopping you from achieving your goal right now?

- ~ Grab a big piece of paper and some coloured pens again.
- ~ Draw on your page four big boulder-like shapes and consider the following labels for each blocker:
    - ~ My thoughts about myself
    - ~ My knowledge, skills or experience gaps
    - ~ Circumstance or situation
    - ~ Feedback from others.

For each boulder theme, spend some time reflecting and being honest about your perception of these. It's important to separate what your thoughts are about yourself and the feedback from others. One is your internal voice; the other is the opinions and feedback from other people. Try to use trusted sources of feedback – people who you feel want to help you challenge yourself to grow.

Take your time working on each of these blockers and write freely what you believe to be reflections of your challenges.

When you are ready, come back and read on.

OK, so here are your blockers. I like to visualise these as boulders of a wall, mostly because I love the image of being able to smash these down into fragments! I think you might also like this analogy too.

Look at each of these boulders and what they symbolise, and consider how they represent the challenges on your pathway.

What I want you to do is take each one in turn (refer to the name you have given this blocker or challenge). I am particularly keen for you to smash down anything within your blockers that are 'self-limiting beliefs'. (This is why I said keep your thoughts separate from the opinions of others.)

My guess is that you might be overly critical of yourself. You may even present some typical imposter syndrome feelings. If so, you should consider how you might rephrase the 'I'm not experienced enough' into 'I'm excited to learn and grow more each day'.

Look at each of your blockers and give additional context on exactly what this blocker/challenge is, its root cause, or where it presents itself as an obstacle on your path.

For example, you may say that lacking confidence is a blocker, so to break this down further you might say:

Lacking confidence – Where do I see this?

- ~ Fear of speaking up and sharing ideas in case they sound ridiculous
- ~ Public speaking makes me feel nervous
- ~ I haven't had much experience to demonstrate the skill
- ~ I feel overshadowed by others who I see to be confident
- ~ I don't feel listened to or appreciated.

Once you have completed this first step, it's **very** important to revisit what you have identified and consider whether these statements or notes are based on fact or feeling. What do you **know** to be true, versus what is a real development need?

Lacking confidence – Where do I see this?

- ~ Fear of speaking up and sharing ideas in case they sound ridiculous *(I know my ideas are well respected)*
- ~ Public speaking makes me feel nervous *(It's not my comfort zone, but I could get better at this)*

- I haven't had much experience to demonstrate the skill *(If I had more opportunity to demonstrate the skills then I know I would feel more confident in my ability)*
- I feel overshadowed by others who I see to be confident *(I wonder how I can learn or leverage from their techniques – maybe they could help me?)*
- I don't feel listened to or appreciated *(Actually, I am by some people, but for others, what ways have I tried to communicate, who do I want to communicate with?)*

Solution Mode

Do you see how in identifying each blocker, I'm beginning to process what could help and support me with it? It's all about balance. If I know how to diagnose the challenge, then at the same time I can start to consider what the appropriate remedy might be.

Don't panic! It is unlikely you will have answers for everything here. There are some things that need time for situations to play out. But what you can do is prepare yourself for overcoming and strengthening what is within your gift to do so.

It is equally important and relevant to keep referring to your strengths. Which of these will help drive you through these blockers and help you navigate ideas for solutions?

If some challenges seem too difficult to navigate, you might want to ask yourself how motivated or driven you are to overcome this right now. Focus on what you **want** to work on, and what you feel is really connected with who you want to be in the future. When it comes to timings, I will always challenge my clients with, 'If not now, then when?'

I know that sometimes timing isn't right, and in exceptional circumstances this is very true. If you are literally about to give birth to your child, then yes, perhaps now is not the time you want to begin studying towards your next qualification! But then again, for some people, this is exactly the time they want to do this.

Be mindful that putting things off until 'the time is right' means it's likely to never be achieved, and maybe it's just not that important to you after all. This is absolutely fine, by the way. I've come to understand that we prioritise and make space for what we truly believe is important right now, and what serves us. If you have aligned your aspirational goal to your strengths, then you are far more motivated to **want** this, and achieve this, right?

I've created a checklist of considerations and questions you can ask yourself the next time you are faced with a challenge you wish to overcome:

Challenge-busting Checklist

☐ **Identify the blockers**

☐ **Are there any self-limiting beliefs?** Are they based on fact or feeling? What evidence do you have to support these beliefs? If none, maybe probe further about what makes you feel less confident in your ability. Why is there doubt etc?

☐ **Knowledge, skills or experience gaps.** What do you need to do the job you want? Who possesses these currently? What is your relationship like with them? Are there other people you could connect with?

☐ **Are you at the right place in your life to progress forward with this?** What else is holding you back? Are there ways to overcome it, now or in the future?

☐ **When was the last time you actively sought feedback about this?** Do people know that you want to develop and progress? What kind of conversations need to happen?

☐ **How are you currently performing?** What perception of you do others have?

Critical Conversations

Whilst I realise this is a powerful self-coaching tool, it doesn't mean you can't share your thoughts and ideas with others. It might be at this stage that you want to talk to your line manager, coach or peers about what you see the challenge to be, and where you feel you can overcome it.

You may be surprised that by sharing this insight into your career goal, that there could be people in your network who are willing to help you work on it.

I recommend seeking some feedback too, particularly if your blockers are regarding a skill you want to develop. This insight from your peers or colleagues can be so valuable. (Unless you work with them, as wonderful as partners, family and friends are, they simply can't give you this type of feedback as they know a version of you that is very different to the 'work you'.) You need to understand how your current performance is being perceived, so you will want to be in a place of welcoming open feedback too.

A professional mentor could also really help. If you have identified experience and knowledge gaps, consider someone who you believe possesses the missing pieces for you. They will be able to share the wonderful gold dust of how they came to understanding and demonstrating this as a strength.

Once you have broken down each blocker in all its glorious detail, you will be left with some considerations, which will likely be in the form of (although not an exhaustive list):

~ Training or upskilling needs
~ Research for you to find out more
~ Studying towards qualifications
~ Broadening your professional network
~ Stretching your skills by trying out a new project or responsibility
~ Reaching out to ask for support or seeking a mentor
~ Having honest conversations and gathering feedback
~ Allocating more time to self-reflect and focus
~ Making a further commitment to self-development, mindfulness or well-being.

Chapter Reflections

Writing down the realities of your situation and what your blockers represent can be a liberating activity. Especially as this can be the time where you can talk yourself out of pursuing your dream as, at first glance, there might be too much standing in your way!

After facing these challenges head on, it's often surprising how quickly they can be broken down.

Casting your light onto that big scary shadowy figure now shows it to be nothing more than a bathrobe hanging off the door. Now that you can identify it, this might not make you jump out of your skin next time!

Now you have identified your blockers and broken them down further, what would you like to do about them?

Just like the bathrobe analogy, you have a few choices. You can acknowledge them and leave them. You could hide from them and pretend they aren't there. You could shine a light on them, move them or wear them.

When it comes to your own career blockers, what could you do and what are you willing to do to overcome these?

Now that you are gathering momentum and have started to consider what solutions you might want to implement, let's skip on through to the Growth section with a sense of accomplishment and pride!

REPOSITION OBSTACLE BLOCKS TO BE
OPPORTUNITY STEPPING STONES...

Chapter 6

G = Growth:

Turning Obstacles into Opportunities

I love this stage of the coaching model. It is where I get to see how my clients want to shape their future. They are often surprised at themselves for seemingly having all the answers within the whole time. We all do really, though sometimes we need a bit of help unlocking them or bringing them to the surface. Once they are at the forefront of our minds and we give them more consideration, our brains quickly start to find patterns and trends in trying to solve the problem.

Self-reflection joins the stage again here. Sometimes we can become overwhelmed with solutions and ideas can go into overdrive. So, if this is you, don't forget to take some time and space to just let these thoughts and ideas simmer. Come back refreshed and with new insight to look again. What seemed to be the obvious solution or workaround may be achieved in another way.

My clients often thrive in this space and their excitement ramps up another gear. I am hoping that some of this is now resonating with you too. You might be beginning to see a plan forming and, by the end of this chapter, will be clear on what opportunities for your own development and growth could look like.

Growth – Is it as Easy as it Sounds?

Having a growth mindset is often something we like to believe we possess, much like feeling accepted and ready for change, but occasionally we have a stark realisation that we don't, at least not as we thought.

It's mostly about comfort zone and how much you want to challenge yourself. Stretching to the unknown and unfamiliar, it's how you feel and where you let anxiety or excitement take control.

Incidentally, it's funny how when we feel anxious our body tells us. It gives us the symptoms, and for each of us this can vary, but we often feel sick, have butterflies in our tummy, become hot, start sweating, need to rush to the toilet, experience a sensation of a dry mouth or a racing heartbeat. Now, if we think about when we feel excited, we often feel these exact same things – feeling sick, having butterflies, becoming hot, starting to sweat, needing the toilet, experiencing a dry mouth or a racing heart. **The same!**

The difference is the association – the mindset and the conditioning we mentally apply.

'I'm calling this feeling *anxious* because I'm feeling nervous and worried about what happens next.'

Versus

'I'm calling this feeling *excitement* because I'm feeling curious and hopeful about what happens next.'

If we think more about growth, a person with a growth mindset will tend to focus on learning and growing, seeing failures as learning opportunities and be willing, even pushing themselves regularly, to go outside of their comfort zone. I am inviting you to start thinking from this place.

Thinking 'Growth'

Let's start thinking about the obstacles as holding the key to achieving success. Rather like stepping stones across a stream. You may need to approach these to overcome this part of the journey. You have smashed through those beastly boulders with force and broken them down into smaller-sized challenges. What is this now telling you?

In the last exercise, you would have been thinking about ideas on what each of these challenges are, where they are identified, and maybe even whether they are self-limiting beliefs or development areas for your own personal or professional growth.

REPOSITION OBSTACLE BLOCKS TO BE OPPORTUNITY STEPPING STONES...

Start now to think about each one in turn in much greater detail, like you are picking up one stepping stone at a time. If it helps you to focus and prioritise these challenges in order of importance or urgency, then do so, but ensure you allow yourself time to review them all. These are the challenges you have identified on the pathway to your aspirational goal, so each one deserves your time and attention.

Using this next technique, you will consider how each of these challenges can be transformed and flipped into opportunities instead. You will be thinking about what you need to do, to turn these obstacles into skills to help you.

Seeing Change or Challenge as Opportunity

We like familiarity, don't we? We like to feel we are assured and certain, confident and comfortable with where we are. It gives us a wonderful sense of stability and knowing. You might be someone who thrives under the pressure of a challenge and enjoys problem-solving. You may be someone who adapts to change very well and demonstrates resilience and a growth mindset. If this is you, **brilliant**! Use this here!

If, however, challenge and uncertainty leave you feeling out of sorts, uncomfortable and a little inadequate, then this will help you through that too. (It's **normal** to start the process of self-development and suddenly become very aware that there are seemingly lots of obstacles.)

Don't be disheartened. The reason I've asked you to spend time getting under the skin of your challenges, is so you can identify them, their importance and weight in your journey and, of course, get you thinking about what can be done. This is a time to consider what you are willing to do. Where there is a will, there is a motivation. I will take you back to the earlier exercise, your Tree of Strength, and your motivation for embarking on this journey in the first place.

Remember the earlier visualisation of successful people? Well, they would have had challenges and obstacles to overcome. It's at this stage that you could shy away and feel this is all too much, that the work ahead is too hard, too great, too long. However, I'll challenge you once more:

~ How much do you really want this?
~ What was driving you in the first place?

Go back to your aim once more (your goal). Connect and feel what it is like for you in that moment, living that life, doing that role, being with those people, in that environment, space, lifestyle, with those values, choices, freedom, talents and strengths.

~ Do you still want that?
~ Are you ready to make it possible?

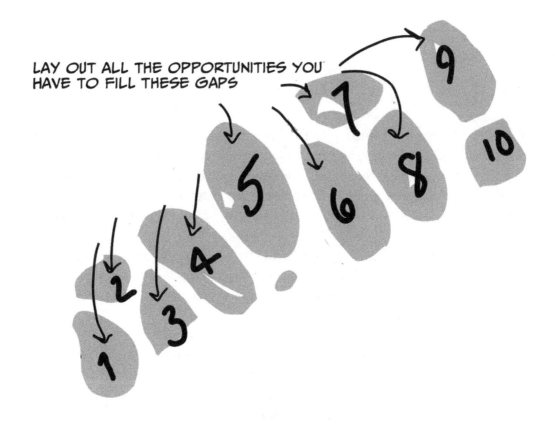

LAY OUT ALL THE OPPORTUNITIES YOU HAVE TO FILL THESE GAPS

The Technique

List all your challenges – then next to each one, list the solutions, remedies or opportunities that can be learning or development steps.

For example, you might say 'lack of experience' is a challenge as you feel there are some knowledge gaps.

So, for the opportunity, you might suggest ways around this to be shadowing a colleague, research, getting closer to projects that would enable experience gain, or seeking a mentor who could help guide you.

I recommend that you change the wording into a positive call to action. So, instead of 'lack of experience', you might wish to rename this 'experience growth'.

Start to order your new growth opportunities. I do this by drawing them out as stepping stones that create a pathway. Number them too, if this helps you. You can, of course, create alternative visuals such as a bridge over a lake, or steps to climb.

You may find some are small 'quick wins', which are easily achieved. Some may take further planning and preparation (particularly if they involve study, training or qualifications), but this is OK, it's all part of your bigger plan!

You may discover that the role you really want could be benefited by you spending time in a 'stop gap' role to broaden and strengthen your skills and experiences.

Now is the time to be honest with yourself and what you are trying to achieve.

Remember it is a journey, so planning the route is essential!

Case Study — Overcoming Challenges

I had been coaching a client for a couple of months when they had reached this stage. The visual techniques had been working very well for them and they were showing an excitement about realising their goal.

They were telling me that reaching their goal may not be simple, and that it involved lots of stages, both known and unknown to them. A little daunted, but hopeful, we looked at the Reality and Growth stages together in the same session.

To their amazement, they found that these challenges were not half as difficult as they had imagined them to be. In fact, they remarked that the steps to solve these and overcome them were quite simple, proudly and confidently declaring, 'Oh, I can definitely do **that**!'

The smile on their face because their dream was possible, and within their own gift, was priceless.

Let this be you too!

Chapter Reflections

Growth is an exciting section of the TARGET model. It is where you faced your blockers head on and called them out. You've given them names and labels, identified how they came into being, and considered how to treat them as opportunities for your own growth.

These are big markers in your journey!

When you adopt this solution-focused mindset, you almost feel invincible. Like anything at all is possible. In truth, most things are possible when we start to consider what we have control of and what our potential could be.

I'm reminded of a time very early in my career when the company I was working for had a change of investors, and with it came additional changes in structure, leadership and process. I'm not adverse to change, in fact I find it quite exciting. At this time, one statement started to resonate with me and is still with me now. 'If we always do what we've always done, we'll always get what we've always got.' This is the challenge a growth mindset will bring. If you want things to remain exactly as they are now and for the next five years, then do nothing, take no action.

Having said this, it is in itself impossible, as we know that nothing lasts forever. Things will always change by some degree. I recently heard an extract from a Wayne Dyer meditation, in which he says, 'you can either live for 90 years or live the same year 90 times'.

It made me think – why would anyone **not** want change?

Undoubtedly, there are things life will throw at us that we have no control over, but we do have control over how we respond to change. This is how I view challenges and, in particular, the ones you will have identified whilst working through this coaching model.

You have within your gift the ability to choose what or how you might overcome the challenges that sit before you. You may be surprised at how easy the solutions are.

I want you to treat yourself to a little celebration at this point. Whether it's your favourite glass of wine, a feel-good movie, or a long soak in the bath. Whatever your little treat when you have something to celebrate, mark this as completing this section.

In the artistic or visual sense, you are creating your pathway, your bridge, or your stepping stone. However you visualised this, it is a way forward. I hope you feel an immense sense of clarity as a result.

I would like you to reflect on these couple of questions as you celebrate this achievement:

- ~ What have you learned most about yourself?
- ~ What one thing will you now do differently?

The next phase of the TARGET model is all about evaluation and, yep, you guessed it, more self-reflection time!

THE JOURNEY I'VE
TAKEN

THE PATH AHEAD

Chapter 7
E = Evaluation:
Taking a Moment to Reflect
on This New Perspective

THE JOURNEY I'VE TAKEN

THE PATH AHEAD

Did you enjoy your little celebratory treat?

Welcome back. This chapter will consider the following two journeys: where you are going to and where you have come from.

I want you to imagine you are on a walking adventure to the top of your mountain, where your destination goal is. This is the time in the long and challenging walk where you come to rest and take stock.

You could be on a small island in the middle of a lake, or at the edge of a forest, or the foothills of your mountain. Wherever this may be for you, I want you to imagine your reflections and begin to evaluate all the learnings so far.

Assess all the beauty that you have uncovered and the strength you have gained from your travels to date.

Think about your strengths you have utilised from the first activity, your Tree of Strength. Are you still motivated and driven by the same things?

Revisit the tree, and feel free to add more talents and skills if you feel you have unearthed these and they are an important factor for you, for future journeys.

Why is Evaluation Important?

It doesn't have to be extensive writing at this stage of the TARGET model, but it is an ideal time to start asking yourself some important questions and understand what your thoughts are right now.

It can be at this part of the journey where you realise you are off course, or your focus goal has moved, or you are energised and the momentum is driving you.

It's easy to get caught up in the tasks of the everyday world and come to a stop when you get here. Remember what I said about self-reflection? I'm giving this to you right now.

I recommend that you embark on your own self-reflection activity here. Now is the time to do this. It's all about perspective and being present.

Be Present in this Moment... Right Now!

Amongst all the thoughts, new ideas and tenacity you are now experiencing, take some time to be still. Allow the quiet ideas time to surface, as well as all the loud and obvious ones that scream at you.

The best way to absorb everything of value is to be present in the moment. Whether this is showing gratitude for the journey, your well-being or freedom, so much time is spent in the space where we imagine all possibilities and focus on the future, that occasionally it helps to recentre and ground ourselves.

I've often found that I tend to get my greatest ideas and alternative 'out-of-the-box thinking' shortly after a brief period of being present in the moment. It is as if this is recharging all of my good stuff, giving an energy boost, plugging into the main power source.

You may notice how you have started to think and feel differently. Maybe others are now noticing this too. You may also start to feel a little drained, that the initial adrenaline rush has run through and you are seeking the next wave. It will come, believe me, it will come.

For now, though, just paddle and float in this little sanctuary, resting here before taking the big push forward.

Here are some typical grounding activities you could try:

- Walking outdoors in the fresh air
- Gardening
- Spending time with family
- Enjoying a good meal
- Socialising with friends
- Listening to music
- Exercising, going to the gym etc
- Going for a drive.

When you are ready, let's pick up again here.

Wow! It already feels like the journey is taking shape. Let's explore and reflect on what has been accomplished to this point.

Taking stock of reserves before the final push is always wise.

For each stage of the TARGET model, you may have created a piece of artwork. All of these are starting to form key components for your big masterpiece. Lay them all out in front of you.

Talent (Your Tree of Strength)

Self-reflect on what is important to you now and in the future. What skills or strengths do you want to develop? What energises you and, ultimately, what do you know you are great at?

Aim – Picturing the Future Goal (Your Mountain)

Visualise and feel what it is like to live and work. What does it really mean to you and what are you willing to do to get there?

Reality (Boulder Blockers)

We have recognised the boulder wall that blocks part of the journey, and whilst some of these boulder blockers appear quite sturdy, we begin to push and break them down. This gives us an indication that perhaps we can repurpose these blocks to help solidify the ground beneath us as we continue with our journey.

Growth (Laying the Pathway)

Select the blocks that will be used as stepping stones for your uneven ground, and understand where opportunities can be sought and created. This is an exciting transformational part of the journey.

It's here where I want you to take a breath. You are not at the point at which you started, but you are also not at the summit of your mountain goal. You are at the edge of the lake. I want you to take some time and reflect on the view and the perspective you have at this stage.

You can decide what tools have served you well so far, what you want to take with you, and reassess the next path you wish to take.

You may have uncovered some steps that you wish to take and are eager to plough on as your adrenaline has kicked in and you're motivated to push forward with this energy. Don't lose this, but before you do run on ahead, spend a few moments reflecting on what this has given you so far.

How has it changed your thinking?

How are you taking accountability for the actions you have created?

Has your end goal moved?

Sometimes, I have found with my coaching clients that we get to this stage and they start to wonder whether their initial goal is still what they want to focus towards, or if it may now be something else. Therefore, I suggest a pause and a reflection at this stage.

You might decide to go back and revisit one of the former stages if your focus has now shifted.

The Technique

I want you to imagine you have a Polaroid camera, and you are taking a photograph of the journey you have had to date, and also a photograph of the journey ahead.

You can create these photographic perspectives however you like; they can be written, in the form of a mind map, drawn, a collage etc.

A sample could look like this:

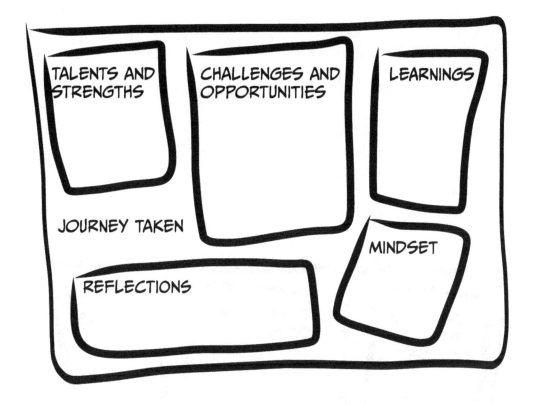

You can think of this as a visual journal, a scrapbook exercise. I want you to think about the headings shown in this image and ask yourself the questions below.

Start creating a visual snapshot of your answers. You can include words and text, doodles, pictures, cuttings etc. Feel free to explore this as artistically as you wish.

Fully immerse yourself in a reflective state of seeing the journey you have travelled; all that you have understood, overcome and learned about yourself so far, and what this experience has given you.

Consider each stage of the model you have completed so far, and use this time to evaluate your understanding and your current awareness.

The Journey So Far (Talent, Aim, Reality, Growth)

~ What have I learned most?
~ What do I now understand about my strengths?
~ What am I motivated by?
~ How do I now view challenges?
~ How do I feel right now?

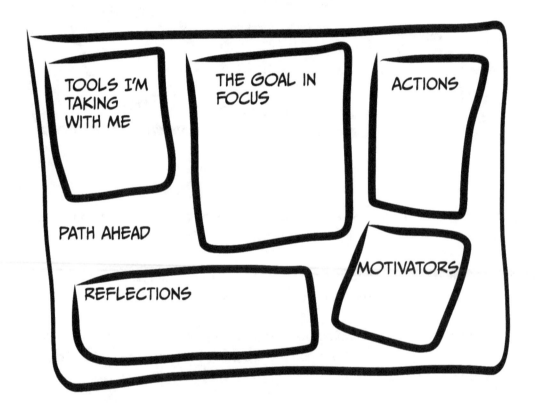

Now do the same for your future vision, the road ahead. I want you to explore how you are viewing your next steps, and how you will use the learning and reflections you have identified to aid you on the rest of your journey.

Consider the headings in the 'Path Ahead' image above and also the questions below.

The Path Ahead

- ~ What will I do next?
- ~ How do I feel about the next steps?
- ~ What key learnings am I taking with me?
- ~ How will I continue to use my drivers and motivators?
- ~ How will I know when I have got to where I want to be?

If you want to draw, doodle or add pictures at this stage, go for it!

As I mentioned earlier, you might be imagining yourself on an island in the middle of a lake, on the outskirts of a forest, or at the base of your mountain, awaiting that final push towards the top.

Whatever images come to you, I encourage you to include these in your snapshots.

Case Study — The Detour

As already detailed, occasionally, a revelation you may encounter when spending time self-reflecting, is one of question and doubt that you are on the right track. This happened to one of my clients, but they were extremely grateful of this realisation, as things worked out for them even better.

My client had an idea of what the next step in his career looked like. For him, there wasn't really a question about it; it was more about timing and when it would manifest itself.

Like many of my willing volunteers to try out an alternative coaching method, this client was more than happy to start at the beginning of my coaching model. He identified his core strengths and talents and, so far, this was aligning well to his goal. We moved through the next couple of stages and all seemed well, but I could see that this individual was perhaps thinking inwardly (internalising). He was focused on the role he thought he should be aspiring to, and less so on the broader options available to him.

An opportunity arose for this client. Seemingly a curveball, something a little out of the blue.

We talked about what resonated with him and how this opportunity aligned with his end goal, and the strengths it could utilise and stretch. Initially, he was thrown off-track by this idea, but I invited him to consider a period of reflection. Based on what he had learned about himself, where he was headed and why he wanted to get to his goal, we discussed his motivation and purpose. What did it really mean to him now?

As it transpired, this new 'curveball' role could offer my client **more** in the way of self-development and professional growth. It was just coming sooner than expected.

A fork in the road like this can leave you feeling one of two things. You can become more determined that you are on the right path (I've seen this experience with another client). Or, it can make you question your sense of direction and prompt you to go back to reviewing what it is you want to do, what skills you want to develop, and where they could take you.

This client is now successfully navigating a very senior position in the organisation. If he had remained blinkered, he may not have seen this fantastic learning opportunity for what it was. Pausing, reflecting and evaluating enabled him to question himself more deeply and envision a new direction he wanted to travel.

Chapter Reflections

At the beginning of this book I talked a lot about the impact of self-reflection. Hopefully, you can now see why this is so beneficial when coaching yourself. It's easy to keep plodding along on life's huge hamster wheel without stopping to take a pause.

I want you to see the value in acknowledging what you have achieved so far and learned about yourself. This part of the TARGET model always seems to promote awareness within my clients, in such a way that they identify their shifts in thinking, since the first activity.

When I ask my clients what has been most impactful at this stage for them, the answers often show as a benefit of focusing on self-development, recognising when it is happening, what triggered it, and how it may form new thinking habits in the future.

One of my clients found that using such creative techniques in coaching could be transferred to other problem-solving and root-cause analysis work in their current role. This is a fantastic learning outcome from this coaching experience.

Another of my clients often felt overwhelmed by choices and options, so the techniques we used in this model helped them to narrow their focus and give their attention and dedication to one objective goal, knowing that other ideas and aspirations were not forgotten, but simply ordered. It stopped them from trying to achieve everything on a small scale, and instead make huge progress on one targeted goal, resulting in a far greater sense of achievement.

Finally, another client found that having visual reference points for each stage of the coaching model helped them recognise their own growth through the process. Keeping these as reference tools helped them pinpoint where or how they wanted to develop, and what their subconscious was telling them through visuals that at times they found difficult to articulate in words.

Whatever your personal take aways from your experiences, make note of these. How you have adapted, found solutions and faced your challenges can also form new ways of working for you in other areas.

I hope you have enjoyed exploring through drawing and illustrating, and that this might be a way to express new learnings in the future.

Keep it going... we only have one more stage of the model to go!

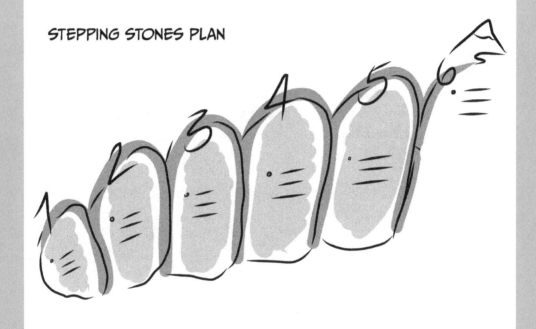

STEPPING STONES PLAN

Chapter 8
T = Timeline:
Stepping Stones and Action Plan

How exciting! Your goal should now feel closer and more possible than before.

You might be thinking to yourself, 'Oh, wow, I **can** actually do this', and you are completely right! It's all down to how you continue to carry that commitment to achieving your goal.

Each stage so far has asked you to visually think about your aspirations with open questions:

- ~ Why? – Your **Talent** (Tree of Strength)
- ~ What? – Your **Aim**
- ~ Where? – Your **Reality** and the challenges right now
- ~ Who and What? – Supports your **Growth** opportunities
- ~ How? – Your **Evaluation** of your experience
- ~ When? – **Timeline!**

Now that you have mastered how to answer all the other questions, this final chapter covers the all-important 'when'.

Why a Timeline or Action Plan is Important to You NOW

What you absolutely do not want to do is let all that creative thinking and visual planning go to waste. Don't let yourself fall into the trap of essentially creating a to-do list, with no fixed end point.

You want to consider all the solutions and options for growth that you have, and be accountable with yourself to make them happen.

Here is where you get to create a timeline, demonstrating the stages of the next steps that you want to accomplish. Each one should be considered, should push and stretch you, and align with your end goal.

Start by simply writing a bullet point list of the actions you want to take, and how you are going to accomplish these. (Don't forget to think about what success feels like for you each time you achieve one of these!)

Now, set yourself realistic deadlines for each one. There might be a specific order you want to commit to, and you may have already identified some 'quick wins'.

You are now ready to formulate these actions into a visual action plan. I use stepping stones or markers on the goal to help with this one.

STEPPING STONES PLAN

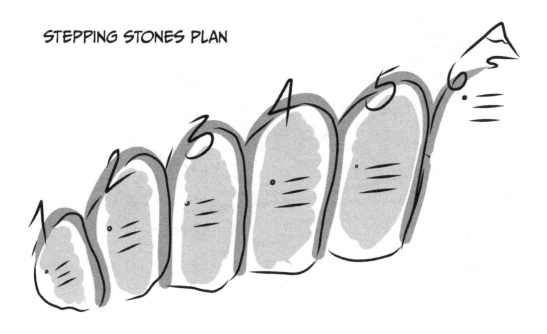

Let's bring back the goal image and start plotting on some markers.

Use the stepping-stone opportunities you identified in the Growth section to plot what these action steps look like on your journey.

This is where it all starts to become a very real commitment from you. Creating an action plan is essentially your big call to action. You need to lead the journey with clarity of the stages and objectives you want to achieve along the way.

You're creating your road map now. You can, of course, create a document or a spreadsheet if you feel more comfortable using these formats to articulate your plan. If you want to keep it visual, here is a format you might want to replicate.

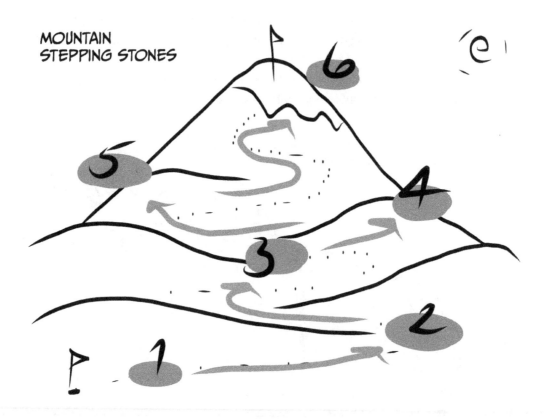

When setting yourself any action plan, you should be realistic with both the timescales and your own expectations. Stretch yourself, that's the whole purpose of self-development, but don't set yourself unrealistic expectations you are unlikely to achieve. Set them because you want them, you will prioritise them, you can relate to them, and because of the strength they will give you.

You will be miserable if you set yourself something you think you should do, but are not engaged to pursue or commit time to doing.

Timeline Action Plan Tips

~ Set yourself realistic actions and time frames.
~ Consider how each action greatly stretches and engages you right now, in the short-term and in the long-term.
~ How will you know when you have achieved the action? What does success look like?
~ Notice any quick wins and celebrate them when they are achieved.
~ Reflect on what you have learned. How has it helped you? Are you now more confident, motivated, excited?

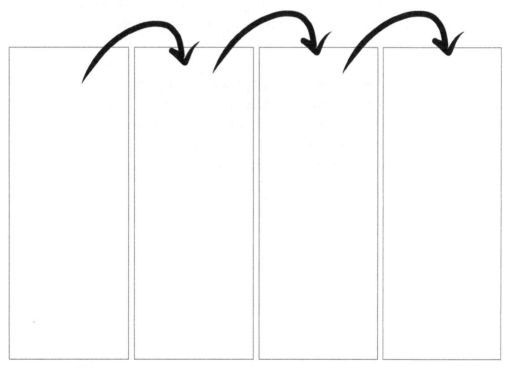

MY ACTION PLAN

So, there you have it, your action plan is complete. How are you feeling about the action steps?

Hopefully you will be feeling charged, energised and ready to get to work on these. You have created a clear path, a way forward, and milestones towards your goal.

Of course, the hard work doesn't stop here. Your commitment and self-drive will be just as critical now as it was before.

There might be times where the road you have mapped out may feel difficult, a struggle even, but this is often when you could be closer to achieving success than you realise. Keep going with it!

If it resonates with your core strengths and purpose, don't let challenge phase you. Remember to keep looking for the opportunity that lies under the surface.

Keep pushing and stretching yourself, but find that balance where you are not too hard on yourself either. Rest is important. Listen to your body when you get those subtle clues that burnout is near, and recognise when you are ignited, empowered and supercharged. When you feel your energy levels lift, identify the feeling as a small part of how it will feel when you reach your end goal.

Your action plan can be shared with key people who can help and support you with the rest of your career pathway. Talk about your plans, why they are important to you, why you are passionate about achieving them, and how they align to your great strengths. Feel confident when you talk about your strengths, as they are your assets, your most valuable tools, so of course you should want to showcase and use them.

Case Study – Share and Impress

I want to share with you this little summary from one of my case studies – a client who had big aspirations of becoming an executive. It didn't take me long to identify that this individual was a visual thinker. By their own admission, they wouldn't often find time to stop and reflect, although they knew passionately the field in which they wanted to work and develop their career.

After working through the first few stages of the TARGET model, I recognised that something special was forming. It was as though they had picked up a pair of binoculars and could see every detail of their goal, and what they could do to bridge the gaps to get there.

When we came to this part, the Timeline, my client shared eagerly all their carefully detailed plans, who could help them get the knowledge and experience they felt was missing, how they were going to learn and upskill, and who else was important to share their timeline with – this, incidentally, had the single largest impact for them on this journey.

Because they were able to articulate with precision where they wanted to get in their career, what they had identified as growth and learning opportunities, and how they planned to make the commitments, their meeting with one of the directors resulted in them being offered a role in the team at an incredibly early stage, much sooner than they anticipated. They had impressed their director with their passion, the time they had taken to reflect properly, and their willingness to share openly their innermost dreams.

I cannot think of a better example of the significance in sharing what you want, with the right people at the right time, after you are 100% clear on your intentions, your own strengths and have faith in your potential.

Chapter Reflections

Congratulations! You've got to the end of the TARGET model. You should now have a clear map ahead for your end goal **and** key markers or stepping stones on how you will get there.

You've achieved this mostly by exploring an alternative method of coaching, which has enabled you to draw or sketch out all the important coaching questions, gain clarity and focus, **and** create unique and stylised artwork in the process. **Wow**!

It's exciting when clients get to this stage, as it feels like they are charged with all the answers and have the momentum to push themselves through to completion. When my clients have got to this point, they share with me how deeply satisfying it feels for them to 'have a plan' to work towards. Even with longer-term goals, you still want to feel like you are moving forward, even if you are in the same role at present.

The difference now is the mindset and the knowledge that you are developing, you are growing, and you are on your way towards something bigger, bolder and more **you**.

Of course, there will be times you experience minor setbacks, but you now have the tools to address these, just like you did when you smashed through your blockers in the 'Reality' task.

The beauty of this model (I say, modestly) is that you can jump back and revisit any section, whenever you need to. You already have all the skills and talent to succeed!

Celebrate when you achieve one of your stepping-stone milestones, it means you are a step closer!

Share with others the journey you are on. You never know, this may open more doors of opportunity. You don't need to fearlessly work through this alone. Seek guidance and support at the sticky stages. You may be surprised at how others can help you in parts of your journey. This has been one of my all-time learnings throughout my own career process.

Summary

Your Big Picture:

Bringing it All Together

Wow – what a journey!

At this point, I invite you to lay out all the component parts of your TARGET plan. This is your narrative to your story towards your career goal.

You now have a choice. You can **either** leave them exactly as they are, as a storyboard of each stage of your process, your key learnings, reflections and discoveries.

~ Your Tree of Strength where your **Talents** are rooted
~ Your **Aim** mountain
~ The boulder wall of your **Reality** challenges
~ Your reinvented pathway of **Growth**
~ Your snapshots as you rested by the lake and **Evaluated** the travelled path or the greater incline ahead
~ Your milestone markers of the achievements and accomplishments you have chosen to include within your **Timeline** to success.

Or, you could construct your original masterpiece by bringing all these components that represent you together into a unique landscape, a self-portrait, a motivational story, a telling piece of illustration.

If you're curious as to how you could make this happen, stick with me and I will go through some simple steps. Alternatively, if you are feeling free and creative, why not make yourself a wonderful abstract one-off piece of expression that captures these components and how you are feeling now. Think about what particularly resonated with you throughout this process and bring it to life through your intuitive mark making. There are no rules. Be free and be you!

Create Your Landscape Masterpiece

What you need:

- ~ A large piece of paper or canvas
- ~ A medium of your choice – paints, pastels, pens, collage etc
- ~ Some of your best creative time – make the space, environment etc exactly to your liking
- ~ Freedom from ego and judgement (it doesn't have to look like a photograph).

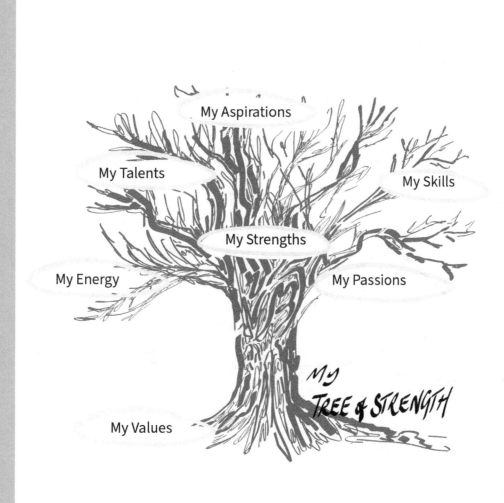

Templates

The Technique

To create the landscape with every component of TARGET, we start with the end in mind. That is, the objects furthest away, in the distance. This will be your mountain.

Before drawing this on the page, if you wish to use some colour for a backdrop, now is the time. You can go with natural tones, such as blue skies and green fields if you wish, or choose colours you are drawn to and go for more of an expressionist approach. Equally, you can leave it plain, should you wish.

I've added a couple of versions here for you, so you get the idea.

See how I have drawn a mountain shape here and some surrounding hillside. You can also gesture the presence of a mountain with colour.

The beauty is that you can use an expressionist approach and gesture the indication of your components; they don't have to be detailed, in proportion, or lifelike, if you don't want them to be. They can be subjective. You know their meaning, but no one else needs to, if you don't want them to.

OK, so our 'Aim' mountains are in place. Let's start to build up some other elements in our picture.

Let's put the 'Tree of Strength' at the front. You can draw this with line making, or just gesture with colour. Here are a couple of versions:

Include that cobbled boulder wall just behind our tree, maybe with a gap in the wall, so you can start to indicate a pathway.

I like a curved pathway, but you can choose how you want to represent this.

That's our reality blockers and our growth opportunity in there.

Remember I referenced a lake? Maybe now is the time to add this in. Indicate this halfway between your tree at the front and the mountain in the distance. It's here where you spent time reflecting on your journey.

Add in some details if you wish, perhaps tall forest trees, an indication of a bridge, or a little rowing boat. These might represent milestone marker points on the way to reaching your mountain goal.

Include any other details you want to introduce, such as birds, clouds, trees, leaves, hedges.

You will see that I've used marks that mostly suggest these are present. I haven't gone into intricate detail, but it can still look effective as a compilation.

If you want to add in some texture, light and shade, consider where you want the sunlight to be and where it would cast its bright beams of light. Add in with white or yellow colour to indicate this, as I have on the previous page.

Similarly, you might consider where there will be natural shadows and darker areas of the picture.

If you are someone who likes to add words to artwork, then do so. You can make them obvious and clear, or perhaps hide the words in the tree bark or the rocks, which you will notice if you look closely.

Maybe there's a particular affirmation that resonates with you. If so, add that in. Let it be something motivational, positive and uplifting.

Every piece of artwork should contain the artist's signature, so sign your name in your work. It is an original and unique piece, crafted by you! Step back and take it all in. You've done it… you've created your masterpiece! You have designed your own destination, built from your core strengths and talents, and mapped your way around challenges, created solutions and presented a clear view to your end goal. Success!

If you have enjoyed creating this, why not play around with other versions. Perhaps a surrealist style such as Salvador Dali, pop art like Andy Warhol, or abstract like Picasso?

Play, experiment and have fun!

Final Self-assessment Activity

- ~ How did you find the activity of bringing together all your TARGET components and creating your 'Big Picture'?
- ~ How might you use these techniques again?
- ~ What have you enjoyed the most from the experience?
- ~ What had the most impact?
- ~ What challenged you the most, and why?
- ~ What are you feeling now?

You have earned yourself time for quiet reflection to take it all in before you start the next exciting phase of your career adventure. Consider the questions above and how you might answer these.

You may find it cathartic to write your answers to the questions as full sentences. For example:

- ~ I found creating my big picture artwork gave me…
- ~ I can see myself using these visual techniques when…
- ~ The thing I most enjoyed about this whole experience was…
- ~ I found the activity that had the most impact on me was…
- ~ I felt challenged the most by…
- ~ I felt this because…
- ~ I am now feeling…

Another option to writing out these sentences is, yes, you might have guessed, to create a visual illustration mind map. Why not? I would!

However, you may want to reflect at this time, and do so at your leisure. There's no rush. The important thing here is to recognise what this whole coaching model has given you that perhaps you didn't have before, or didn't realise you could utilise to get to this point.

TARGET Model Complete

Thank you for exploring your career journey through this art-based model. I hope by doing so, it has helped you to try out new techniques for self-coaching.

Your Learnings

I am always interested to hear about the big learnings my clients take away from using this model. I'm keen to hear about how you found this too! If you are happy to share your insights, please visit my website www.richanah.co.uk or email me at info@richanah.co.uk and let me know what you took away from this process.

I would love to see some of your visual creations and representations!

Feel free to subscribe to my mailing list on the website, if you wish to follow me and hear about other exciting new projects I am working on.

My Story

Driven by Adversity and Life Learnings:

Experiencing Setbacks and Sharing My Dreams with Others

I recently had a dream (though not as profound as Martin Luther King, of course). Nevertheless, a dream is a dream.

I wanted to deepen my knowledge of coaching for my own professional development, but also because I knew it was something I was passionate about. I've journeyed a little in my career to date, always feeling like I had missed an opportunity somewhere. Well, I know I haven't, as I am a believer in whatever is intended for you, will not pass you by.

I am full of these spiritual affirmations; they represent my go-to positive mind talk. I also trust my intuition.

I've always had a connection with creativity and art. I studied this at college and had my sights set on becoming a designer, or even a children's book illustrator. I had been accepted into Birmingham University when I was 19 and was ready to embark on the journey.

This was back in 2003, the year that a series of tragedies befell my family. My older sister passed away in the April through natural causes. She was born with spina bifida, but she achieved far and beyond what medical professionals had anticipated. I witnessed my Dad break down and apologise to me for it, as he tried to find the words to commemorate his final goodbye on his note on the flowers. This was my first big learning about the strength in vulnerability.

Then, in August of that year, a tragedy occurred that is vividly imprinted on my mind. We found out that my older brother had taken his own life. Crushed, devastated, disbelief. I'm not sure there's a word that exists to describe the pain of seeing your parents grieve having lost a child. My Dad lost his daughter and my Mom had lost her son, all within a few months. It was truly the darkest time I have witnessed.

I had no idea that my brother lived with depression. No idea at all. It's always those with the brightest smile who carry the most sadness. This I have learned as the years pass by. I was aware though that no one should feel like they are alone and cannot confide in anybody.

Another realisation struck me during this time, which has stayed with me ever since. This was the ultimate benchmark of strength and despair, all at once. If I can get through this, nothing that life throws at me can measure with what this feels like.

The summer of 2003 made me stop and assess my purpose in life and what I wanted to do. I had been offered a job based at the NEC in Birmingham, designing floorplans for trade shows and exhibitions. This was at the same time as being accepted into university. Right then, something made me consider the path I would choose. I can't explain why, but I was being drawn towards taking the job, over continuing my further education. I wanted to buy a property and I had fierce aspirations to create a life where I was happy and excited for the future.

My focus for work at this incredibly difficult time was, and has been ever since, the driver for stability and control. It was also through a fierce stubbornness and sheer will that I was going to make what I wanted happen. I couldn't change the past, I could only encourage the future to take the shape I wanted it to. So, I started my job the following week and began to save for my first house soon afterwards.

In the meantime, I had adventures. I travelled on some wonderful holidays and explored lots of places I had dreamed of. I was embracing 'living in the moment'.

A few years passed and, aged 22, I purchased my first house, whilst also achieving many things along the way.

I'm not sure whether I would have made the same choices had the summer of 2003 been different. What I do know, though, is it triggered an empathy for others within me that has never gone away, and a desire to support the development of other people and help them recognise and support their own talents.

I got married and started a family. The travel and daily commutes into the city and out the other side began to take toll and made me question my values as a new mother. I went back to work after just three months on maternity leave. I could not afford to take more time off with only maternity pay (one third of my monthly salary).

After 12 months and various challenging commutes, where I was leaving the house before 6am and arriving home after 8pm, missing every mealtime with my son, as well as bath time and bedtime, I decided something needed to change. I needed to find a balance and gain more quality time with my family. So, I took an admin job closer to home and, subsequently, a hefty drop in salary.

An incredibly difficult see-saw of emotions ensued. On one hand I was a present parent, but on the other, I felt I had completely lost my identity for relinquishing my talents and skills into something I knew, deep down, was not what I really wanted to do. I was doing the right thing but was feeling miserable. Yet something within told me this was not the right time; stick with it and, at some stage, there will be opportunity to grow again. I had been through a lot worse and was very lucky in many ways.

Right now, my focus was not on my career.

I soon had opportunities in different roles within the organisation, and started to learn more about the business from different perspectives. I was beginning to recognise where others were seeing my value and wanted more of my input. It was fantastic!

It wasn't that long before I had the opportunity to lead a team. Here, I understood the importance of using leadership skills to empower and enhance the development of others. I learned a lot about leading teams during this time, small teams and large teams. I kept coming back to this feeling of huge achievement and value when working with others to help them achieve their goals. I loved connecting with people, facilitating training sessions, discussions, problem-solving, team-building days etc. Exploring the potential in others was definitely 'my thing'. The only thing that was missing was using my artistic skills – though I tried to sneak these in at every opportune moment!

As soon as the opportunity arose within the Learning and Development team, I knew I had arrived home. It was a place where I could be creative **and** work with my other core strengths.

However, this is all just the backdrop. The main part of me sharing my story is the most recent learning I have experienced following my dream.

I was coaching people in my Learning and Development role. I loved being in this space, but I felt there was more to this than I was currently giving (a similarly intuitive feeling I have had before). I wanted to go bigger, bolder and reach more people.

What I did this time, which I hadn't done before, was start to share my dream with others; my line manager, coach, peers and friends. It was as though the more I started to talk about it, the more energy it was creating.

My dream was to write a book about a creative coaching model where I combine art and coaching, and help others to explore an alternative approach to unlocking all the mind fuzz, recognise where they are powerful, and use these strengths to drive them towards the greatness they are searching for.

At first, I was immensely aware that I felt out of my depth. There were others more experienced within coaching; who am I to think I can write a book?

But then, my coaches were asking me in response:

- Do you have your own ideas?
- Who are you **not** to write a book and share these?

From this moment, I've been sharing, and what has happened since has been remarkable. I have been privileged to connect with some exceptional professionals within the coaching and publishing arenas. People who want to help me get this concept into words. People who are interested and have the belief that this is something of relevance and interest.

I'm most definitely working on a different energy level now, and meeting so many inspirational, exciting and knowledgeable people. **This** feels like the intention. **This** feels like what I was meant to do. Everything leading up to this has given me fantastic learning and insight about myself, and belief in my own potential.

If there are people in your network and you have been hesitant or reluctant to share or involve them in your dream, tell them! Allow them to help you. If you are like me, this will feel uncomfortable at first, but allowing yourself to feel vulnerable and scared in front of others also helps you become stronger and more resilient. Genuinely, people want to help you; they feel honoured to be invited in by you, so don't hold back. You don't have to be a hero and go it alone. Vulnerability is welcome in a supported environment. My two earlier life lessons come back and get replayed again.

I've learned how to manage setbacks and accept them for what they are. There have been times where I have felt disheartened or cannot understand why things didn't work out at that time. There will be another way, another route.

I don't lose faith, and neither should you. If it feels right, and aligns with your passions and strengths, then keep going. It will all come in divine time.

Remember from someone who knows – what is intended for you will not pass you by!

About the Author

Richanah Daly is a professional coach and artist who combines her experience from the last 10 years of leading and developing others with her talent for illustration, to create a unique and powerful approach to coaching, blending self-reflection, mindfulness techniques and art together to enable her clients to create their own masterpieces of discovery.

As an experienced Learning and Development partner within a market-leading property management organisation, she has focused on developing early careers and graduate programmes for emerging leaders of the future, in addition to her wider coaching practice.

Richanah studied Advanced Art and Design and then a Diploma in Foundation Studies, specialising in narrative illustration. She began her career with a worldwide award-winning event management company, designing floorplans for trade shows and exhibitions to make her clients' vision come to life.

A practising spiritual artist for the last 20 years, Richanah uses visual aids as a powerful tool to connect with others more deeply. Through this practice, she has developed tools for representing self-reflection more powerfully in visual form, which forms a key part of her ongoing professional coaching research.

Richanah has an Etsy shop which showcases her hand-created artwork. She is also an active member of an 'On Your Doorstep Virtual Mall' which promotes local craft businesses, and during the recent pandemic shared printable illustrative mindfulness activities for children through social media.

More recently, Richanah has been working on her own brand of Creative Coaching and Consultancy, where she has been supporting clients with their learning programmes, in addition to working on commissions for children's book illustrations.

Website: www.richanah.co.uk

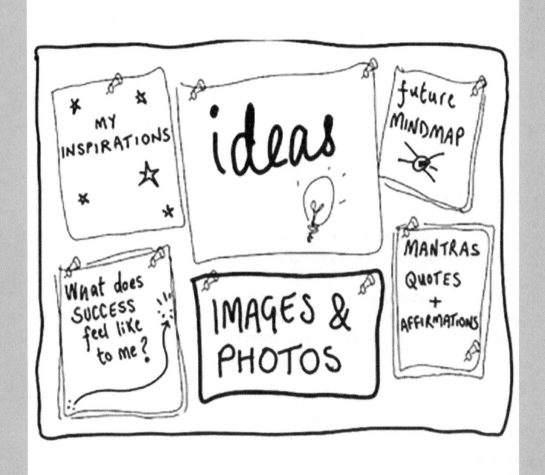

Acknowledgements

I have been extremely blessed to have had such a wonderful tribe of support and encouragement with me on this awesome journey. People who truly valued what I could bring, my strengths and potential, and who embraced me for all that I am. Their unwavering support could not go unmentioned, and of course it is the reason why I am so passionate about coaching others to play to their strengths and explore their own passions, just as they did with me.

Emma and Carl – Both fantastic coaches who I have learned from and who have helped me learn even more about myself, and who enabled me to put the imposter syndrome clone back in her box, have faith and keep exploring the magic of what I imagine!

Shirley and Diane – For allowing me a platform to explore and share, to try out new things and cheer me on along the way.

Alison – The guidance from her expertise has been outstanding. I went from having an idea to becoming an author with her wisdom!

Bitesh – My mindset guru. The one who challenged my way of thinking about my potential and what could be possible if I allowed myself to push, embrace the challenges and take all the learnings as strengths.

My wonderful TARGET model subjects – A fabulous and trusting group of individuals who were more than willing for me to try out something brand new with them. Thank you, Adil, Ollie, George, Jas and Jane. Their open minds to explore alternative techniques, feedback and insight has been so inspiring. I've loved watching how each of their journeys have unfolded over our sessions, and it's been a real pleasure to have seen their goals come to reality.

Feedback from a mixture of professional coaches (too many to list) – For their support in virtual masterclasses, surveys, insights, followings and all their likes and shares! They all helped me gather the value to bring this to life.

Inspirations:

~ GROW model
~ Ishikawa
~ Instant Pay-off Coaching
~ Strengthscope® profiling
~ Myers-Briggs Personality Profile
~ Mindfulness
~ Jim Carrey story.

CPSIA information can be obtained
at www.ICGtesting.com
Printed in the USA
LVHW061346200722
723788LV00009B/285